KNOPF MAPGUIDES

Welcome to Dublin!

This opening fold-out contains a general map of Dublin to help you visualize the 6 districts discussed in this guide, and 4 pages of valuable information, handy tips and useful addresses.

Discover Dublin through 6 districts and 6 maps

A Medieval City / Liberties
B Temple Bar / Trinity College / Kildare Street
C St Stephen's Green / Merrion Square / Grand Canal
D O'Connell / IFSC
E Glasnevin / Parnell / Phoenix Park
F Smithfield / St James / Kilmainham

For each district there is a double-page of addresses (restaurants – listed in ascending order of price – cafés, bars, tearooms, music venues and shops), followed by a fold-out map for the relevant area with the essential places to see (indicated on the map by a star ★). These places are by no means all that Dublin has to offer, but to us they are unmissable. The grid-referencing system (**A** B2) makes it easy for you to pinpoint addresses quickly on the map.

Transportation and hotels in Dublin

The last fold-out consists of a transportation map and 4 pages of practical information that include a selection of hotels.

Index

Lists all the street names, sites and addresses featured in this guide.

LITERARY DUBLIN

Since the 17th century, Dublin has inspired some of the world's greatest writers (and built up statues in their honor): Swift, Stoker, Wilde, Joyce, O'Flaherty, Behan, O'Brien. Four Nobel prizewinners were Dubliners: Beckett, Heaney, Shaw and Yeats.
James Joyce Museum
→ Sandycove, Dun Laoghaire; Sandycove Dart stop. Tel. 280 9265 Mon-Sat 10am–1pm, 2–5pm; Sun 2–6pm (Nov-Feb by appt)
In the Martello Tower, which was the original starting point for Ulysses' journey.

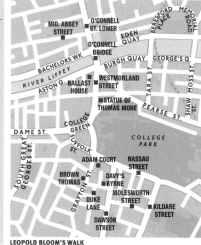

LEOPOLD BLOOM'S WALK

lectures, performances.
July-August
Summer Festival
→ Tel. 605 7700
Free concerts in the parks.
Failte Ireland Horse Show
→ Beg. Aug, for five days; www.dublinhorseshow.com
Horse fair.
October
Dublin Theatre Festival
→ First two weeks; www.dublintheatrefestival. com
Major shows from Ireland and all over the world.

BUDGET

Eating out in Dublin isn't particularly cheap but staying in a hotel or even a B&B *is* expensive.
Accommodation
A double room in the city center: from €80 (hotel), and €40 (*guesthouse*) .
Restaurants
The bill
Unless otherwise stated,

prices indicated in this guide are for an à la carte evening meal and include a starter, a main course and a drink. For lunch allow €10 to €20, and often twice that amount for dinner.
The tip
Fifteen percent service is added to your bill, but it is usual to add a little extra on top (5 to 10% of the total).
Going out
A beer in Temple Bar: €5–6 (€3–4 outside the center). Entrance to a nightclub: €5–20. A show at the Abbey Theatre: €15–30.
Museums
Entry to the national museums is free. Elsewhere, allow €5–10.

GETTING AROUND

The Liffey cuts the city in two: north bank and south bank. There are 24 postal districts: odd numbers in

the south and even numbers in the north, starting at the river. The Grand Canal and the Royal Canal form the outer limits of the city.

OPENING TIMES

Museums
→ Usually 10am–5pm/ 6pm. Closed Sun and/or Mon. Restricted opening times in winter.
Restaurants
→ Usually noon–2.30pm, 6–11pm. Non-stop service in pubs and cafés.
Traditional pubs
→ As a rule pubs close at 11pm/11.30pm on Sun-Wed, and at 12.30am on Thu-Sat.
Late bars
→ Most stay open from Thu until 1.30/2.30am, but a few close at 3 or 4am.
Shopping
→ Mon-Sat 9.30am–6pm (late-night opening until 8pm on Thu.

ARCHITECTURE

Medieval Anglo-Norman style
Mostly religious buildings remaining, in Early English style (12th c.), St Patrick's (**A** D4) and St Audoen's (**A** C2).
Georgian style (1715–1830)
Classical lines based on designs from antiquity. Pediments, carving and columns. Famous architects include James Gandon (1743–1823): Custom House (**D** B4). But also the Francini Brothers: Tyrone House (**D** B3), Thomas Cooley: City Hall (**A** F2) and Richard Cassels: Leinster House (**B** E3).
Victorian style (1830–1900)
Still some Georgian elements, this was the high point of neo-styles: Christ Church Cathedral (**A** D2): neo-Gothic. Heuston Station (**F** C2): neo-Renaissance station Beginnings of the Industrial Age with the Guinness storehouse (**F** D2).
Dublin houses
Brick, slate and ornamental ironwork are typical of Georgian and Victorian styles here. Brightly-painted front doors, with elegant fanlights above, Merrion Square (**C** D2).
Modern architecture and contemporary styles (20th–21st c.)
Modern complexes include the Berkeley Library (**B** D2) in Trinity College. Contemporary styles a strong feature of the IFSC (**D** C4).

CITY PROFILE

- Capital city of the Republic of Ireland since 1922 ■ 1.1 million inhabitants
- 44 square miles
- Over 6.5 million visitors every year
- Over 1,000 pubs
- Official languages: English and Gaelic
- Time zone: GMT, except in summer when the time is shifted forward by one hour
- Climate: temperate. Temperatures: **April:** min. 4°C/39°F, max. 12°C/54°F; **Aug:** min. 11° C/52°F, max. 19°C/ 66°F; **Dec:** min. 3°C/ 37°F, max. 8°C/46°F.

ARRAN QUAY, ALONG THE LIFFEY

WWW.

Websites
General information
→ *www.visitdublin.com*
→ *www.dublin.ie*
→ *www.dublintourist.com*
Internet cafés
Central Café (**B** C3)
→ *6 Grafton St*
Tel. *677 8298*
Right Click (**C** B3)
→ *70 Lower Camden St*
Tel. *475 9681*

TOURIST OFFICES

Dublin Tourism Centre (**B** B2)
→ *Suffolk St. Tel. 605 7745 Mon–Sat 9am–5.30pm (7pm July-Aug); Sun 10.30am–3pm*
In a former church: leaflets and brochures, car rental, hotel reservations.
Other tourist offices
→ *Arrival Hall, Dublin Airport*
→ *14 O'Connell St Upper* (**D** A3)
→ *Baggot St Bridge* (**C** E3)

TELEPHONE

USA / UK to Dublin
Dial 011 (from the USA) / 00 (from the UK) + 353 (Ireland) 1 (city) + local 7-digit number.
Dublin to USA / UK
Dial 00 1 (USA) / 44 (UK) + area code (minus the 0 for UK numbers) + number.
From outside Dublin to Dublin
Dial 01 + local 7-digit number.
Within Dublin
Dial Dial 01 + local 7-digit number.
Emergency numbers
Police, emergencies
→ *999 (or 112 from a mobile phone)*
Medical assistance
→ *676 7273*

DIARY OF EVENTS

Public holidays
Jan 1; March 17 (St Patrick, national celebration);
Easter Mon; Easter Fri; May 1 (Labor Day, celebrated on the first Mon in May); first Mon in June (Spring Festival); first Mon in Aug (Summer Festival); last Mon in Oct (Winter Festival, Halloween); Dec 25; Dec 26 (St Stephen's day).

February-March
Dublin Film Festival
→ *Mid Feb, for nine days; www.dubliniff.com*
International film festival of mainstream and independent movies.
St Patrick
→ *Mid March, for five days*
Huge parade with fireworks, giant puppets, Celtic dancing etc.

April-May
International Dance Festival
→ *End April and/or beg. May for one to two weeks; www.dancefestivalireland.ie*
The world's best modern dance companies meet in Dublin; shows throughout the city.

Heineken Green Energy Festival
→ *End April or beg. May*
One-week pop and rock festival with national and international bands.
June-September
Diversions Festival
→ *June-Sep; www.temple-bar.ie*
Free shows and performances on the Temple Bar square: music, theater, dance. The biggest outdoor festival in Ireland.
June
Bloomsday Festival
→ *One week around June 16, www.jamesjoyce.ie*
On June 16, 1904, Leopold Bloom, the hero of James Joyce's *Ulysses*, 'walked out' around Dublin, stopping at 14 different places, all now marked by a plaque. Each year, on this day, Dubliners dress up in costume of the period and recreate this journey. With talks,

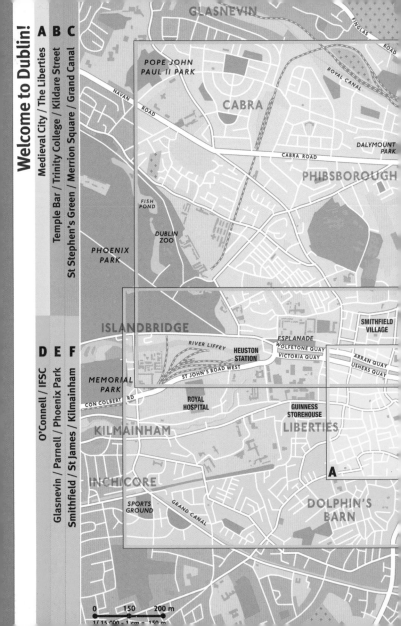

Welcome to Dublin!

A Medieval City / The Liberties
B Temple Bar / Trinity College / Kildare Street
C St Stephen's Green / Merrion Square / Grand Canal
D O'Connell / IFSC
E Glasnevin / Parnell / Phoenix Park
F Smithfield / St James / Kilmainham

GLASNEVIN

FINGLAS ROAD

POPE JOHN PAUL II PARK

ROYAL CANAL

CABRA

NAVAN ROAD

CABRA ROAD

DALYMOUNT PARK

PHIBSBOROUGH

FISH POND

DUBLIN ZOO

PHOENIX PARK

ISLANDBRIDGE

RIVER LIFFEY

HEUSTON STATION

ESPLANADE
WOLFETONE QUAY
VICTORIA QUAY

SMITHFIELD VILLAGE

ARRAN QUAY
USHERS QUAY

MEMORIAL PARK

ST JOHN'S ROAD WEST

CON COLBERT RD

ROYAL HOSPITAL

GUINNESS STOREHOUSE

LIBERTIES

KILMAINHAM

A

INCHICORE

SPORTS GROUND

GRAND CANAL

DOLPHIN'S BARN

0   150   200 m

1/ 15 000 - 1 cm = 150 m

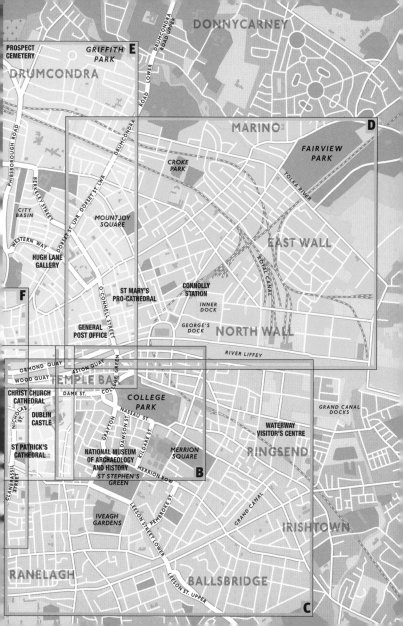

DONNYCARNEY

PROSPECT
CEMETERY

GRIFFITH
PARK **E**

DRUMCONDRA

MARINO **D**

CROKE
PARK

FAIRVIEW
PARK

TOLKA RIVER

PHIBSBOROUGH ROAD

BERKELEY STREET

CITY
BASIN

WESTERN WAY

HUGH LANE
GALLERY

DORSET ST. UPR

DORSET ST. LWR

DRUMCONDRA ROAD LOWER

DRUMCONDRA ROAD UPPER

MOUNTJOY
SQUARE

EAST WALL

ROYAL CANAL

F

O'CONNELL STREET

ST MARY'S
PRO-CATHEDRAL

CONNOLLY
STATION

INNER
DOCK

GENERAL
POST OFFICE

GEORGE'S
DOCK

NORTH WALL

RIVER LIFFEY

ORMOND QUAY

WOOD QUAY

ASTON QUAY

TEMPLE BAR

DAME ST.

CHRIST CHURCH
CATHEDRAL

NICHOLAS ST.

DUBLIN
CASTLE

COLLEGE GREEN

COLLEGE PARK

NASSAU ST.

GRAND CANAL
DOCKS

ST PATRICK'S
CATHEDRAL

GRAFTON ST.

DAWSON ST.

KILDARE ST.

MERRION
SQUARE

WATERWAY
VISITOR'S
CENTRE

RINGSEND

CLANBRASSIL STREET

NATIONAL MUSEUM
OF ARCHAEOLOGY
AND HISTORY

ST STEPHEN'S
GREEN

MERRION ROW

B

IVEAGH
GARDENS

LEESON STREET LOWER

PEMBROKE ST.

GRAND CANAL

IRISHTOWN

RANELAGH

LEESON ST. UPPER

BALLSBRIDGE

C

STATUE OF JAMES JOYCE

TEMPLE BAR MARKET

EXCURSIONS AROUND DUBLIN

perfect place to meet and have a good time (*craic*).

Late bars

From Thursday, bands or DJs usually play until 4am.

Reservations

Ticketmaster (**E** E4)
→ *Jervis Center, Jervis St*
Tel. 456 9569
www.ticketmaster.ie
Reservations on the spot, by telephone or online: plays, concerts and sporting events.

Listings

From newsstands
In Dublin (every fortnight): shows and festivals.
Hot Press (every fortnight): musical news and events.

Free

Dublin Event Guide: detailed listing, twice weekly, available in bars and cafés.

SPORTS

Hurling and Gaelic football

→ *Croke Park Stadium* (**D** C1)

Tel. 819 2300 Reservation from the GAA (Gaelic Athletic Association) (**D** B1) Tel. 836 3222. www.crokepark.ie
The two national sports.

Hurling

A cross between hockey and rugby. Played on a pitch with a leather ball (*sliothár*) and flat wooden bats (*camán*). Thirty players, two teams.

Gaelic football

Very fast football in which you can use your hands as well as your feet.

Hurling and Gaelic football championships

→ *Croke Park www.gaa.ie
Every Sun, May-Sep*
Tickets available from Croke Park, except in September during finals when seats are reserved for clubs' members.

Rugby and football

→ *Lansdowne Rd Stadium
Irish Rugby Football Union
Tel. 647 3800 (the legendary stadium is being renovated*

until 2008; until then most matches are played in Croke Park Stadium)
Buy tickets in advance for major national matches.

Golf

→ *Golfing Union of Ireland
Tel. 505 4000. www.gui.ie*

Horseracing

→ *Leopardstown, Foxrock
Luas (Sandyford stop)
Tel. 289 0500*
Horseracing courses 6 miles southeast of the city center.

Greyhound racing

→ *www.igb.ie*
A local specialty. The greyhounds pursue their prey at over 50mph under the watchful eyes of those who have placed bets.
→ *Shelbourne Park (off **C** F2)
300 yards east of Grand Canal Docks. Tel. 668 3502*
→ *Harold's Cross (off **F** F4)
600 yards south of Grand Canal Docks. Tel. 497 1081*
The city's two greyhound tracks, on the right bank of the Liffey.

EXCURSIONS

Casino at Marino

→ *Malahide Rd. 3 miles from city center. Bus 20, 27, 42, 123 and Dart (Clontarf Rd stop). Tel. 833 1618*
Built by Chambers in 1758, a former summer house now considered to be the finest neoclassical building in Ireland.

Malahide Castle

→ *7 miles from Dublin. Bus 42, 102, 105, Dart and Northern suburban*
Home of the Talbot family (12th c.), with many pictures, antiques, a terrific model railway and superb botanical garden.

Skerries Mills

→ *Skerries; 20 miles. Bus 33 and Northern suburban*
Industrial heritage museum with 17th- and 18th-c. windmills and watermill: fun for all the family.

Ardgillan Castle

→ *Balbriggan ; 24 miles. Bus 33. Tel. 849 2212*
Fine country house (1738) with 200 acres of woodland and gardens overlooking Drogheda Bay.

Howth Peninsula

→ *8 miles from Dublin. Bus 31A/B then Dart*
Attractive walks with great clifftop views and a lighthouse.

Dún Laoghaire

→ *8 miles. Bus 45A, Dart then South East suburban*
Attractive resort town and harbor with classic 19th-c. villas.

Bray

→ *14 miles. Bus 45A, Dart then South East suburban*
A Victorian seaside resort with great sandy beaches. Here too are the aquariums of the National Sea Life Center.

ASON

MERRION SQUARE

THE GROGAN, ONE OF DUBLIN'S THOUSAND PUBS

MUSICAL DUBLIN

Traditional Irish music
Wherever you go in Dublin you will find traditional music – pub gigs and concerts alike.
Gaiety Theatre (**B** B4)
→ *King Street South Tel. 677 1717*
Irish pop-rock
Though many musical styles are represented in Ireland, rock and pop have given the country an international reputation.
Legendary musicians:
U2, Sinead O'Connor, the Cranberries, the Corrs...
Concert halls
Olympia Theatre (**A** F2), Temple Bar Music Centre (**B** A1), etc.

EATING OUT

Daily life
Breakfast: generous Irish breakfast. Around 1pm, light lunch. Dinner is around 6pm or 7pm.
Where to eat
Restaurants
They serve international and local cuisine. Many Italian, French and Asian restaurants have opened in Dublin in the past few years.
Pubs
This is where you can sample Irish fare, such as the Irish stew.
Cafés and tearooms
Open from 8am to 6pm, they serve sandwiches, salads and homemade soups. Often packed at lunchtime.
Specialties
Irish breakfast: fried egg, tomato, sausage, black pudding and brown bread.
Irish stew: lamb stew with

cabbage and potato. Many fish (salmon, cod), seafood (oysters, mussels) and meat (lamb, beef) dishes.
Irish coffee: a mix of black coffee, sugar, whiskey and cream.

BEER AND WHISKEY

Beer
Ireland is famous for its ales (Smithwicks) but even more for its stouts (Murphy's, Guinness, Beamish). The best lagers are imported.
Whiskey
Some of the best known Irish whiskeys are: Bushmills Malt (1608), Powders, Jameson, Paddy's, Midleton, Connemara and Redbreast.

MUSEUMS

Reductions
Many museums offer

discounts to the under 16s and the over 60s.
Guided tours
Historical Walking Tours (B C2)
→ *Depart from Trinity College Tel. 878 0227*
www.historicalinsights.ie
Visits (on foot) organized by history students from Trinity College.
Dublin Bus City Tour (D A3)
→ *59 O'Connell St Upper Tel. 873 4222*
Depart every 10–15 mins, from 9.30am to 5pm.
Discover Dublin onboard a bus in 21 stages (1¼ hrs); ticket valid 24 hrs.

SHOPPING

Sales
First two weeks in January and/or July-Aug. Some stores have sales in April.
Grands magasins
St Stephen's Green Centre (**B** B4)
→ *Grafton St. Tel. 478 0888*

Dunnes Stores (**B** C3)
→ *Grafton St. Tel. 671 4629*
Arnotts (**D** A4)
→ *12 Henry St. Tel. 872 1111*
Easons (**D** A4)
→ *40 O'Connell St Tel. 858 3800*
Clery's (**D** A4)
→ *18-27 Lower O'Connell St Tel. 878 6000*
Jervis Centre (**E** E4)
→ *Jervis St. Tel. 878 1323*
Crafts
Irish tweed and Irish knitwear – all handmade, Celtic jewelry, china and quality Irish crystal (vases, glasses etc.).

NIGHTLIFE

No-smoking law
Smoking has been banned in all public places since 2004.
Where to go
Traditional pubs
Irish pubs, on every street corner, are an institution in their own right and the

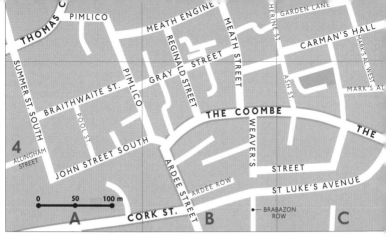

CHRIST CHURCH CATHEDRAL

ST WERBURGH'S CHURCH

A

★ St Patrick's Cathedral (A D4)
→ St Patrick's Close
Tel. 453 9472 Mon-Sat 9am–6pm (5pm Sat in Nov-Feb); Sun 9–11, 1.45–3pm, 4.15–6pm (10–11am, 1.45–3pm in Nov-Feb). Choir evensong at 5.45pm (except Sat)
The largest church in Ireland has stood on this site since 1191, close to the legendary well where St Patrick is said to have baptized the first Catholics. The building served as a university and a stable before being turned into a religious building. There are busts and tombs in homage to great Irishmen – the powerful Boyle family, Swift and his companion, Stella, etc. Don't miss the hole in the north transept door through which the counts of Kildare and Ormond shook hands.

★ Marsh's Library (A E4)
→ St Patrick's Close
Tel. 454 3511
Mon, Wed-Fri 10am–1pm, 2–5pm; Sat 10am–1pm.
www.marshlibrary.ie
Twenty-five thousand works dedicated to the sciences fill the rickety bookshelves, and precious volumes fill three small nooks. This library, founded by Archbishop Narcissus Marsh, has remained intact for 300 years. How? Readers were locked in the nooks behind wire railings to study the rare books.

★ Tailor's Hall (A D2)
→ 8 Back Lane. Tel. 454 1786
Visits by appointment
The only guildhall (1706) still standing in Dublin. In 1792 it became the meeting place of the Irish Unionists, who would gather in the basement room – hence its nickname Back Lane Parliament. Today it houses the National Trust for Ireland, An Taisce.

★ St Audoen's (A C2)
→ High St
Tel. 677 0088 (Protestant church)
June-Sep: daily 9.30am–5.30pm
Two churches, one Catholic the other Protestant, both dedicated to St Ouen tower of the latter chu the older (12th c.), are three oldest bells (14 Ireland.

★ Dublinia (A D2)
→ St Michael's Hill
Tel. 679 4611 Daily 10a Oct-March: Mon-Fri 11a 4pm; Sat-Sun 10am–4
Entertaining trip thro Viking Dublin: a mod the city, waxworks, vi and objects. Remains in the Wood Quays complete the picture: cauldrons, pots, frag and teeth. At the top St Michael's Tower, o vestige of a 12th-cen church, there are stu views of the city. Fro

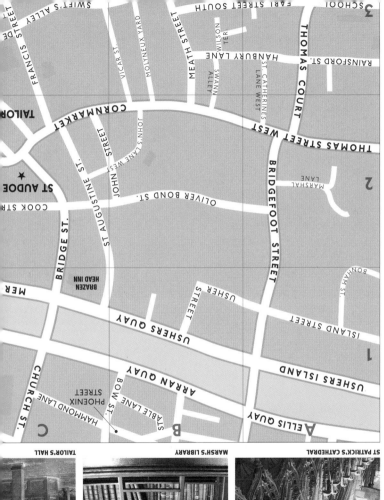

TAILOR'S HALL

MARSH'S LIBRARY

ST PATRICK'S CATHEDRAL

The Liberties district, running from the Liffey to Cornmarket, stands outside what were once the limits of the old Viking settlement. Anglo-Norman churches and cathedrals rise up above the medieval city, a place of crumbling façades and antiquated pubs from which, for hundreds of years, the sound of laughter, song and the clinking of glasses have escaped. Around Thomas Street a series of inexpensive stores, a row of antique shops and a maze of tiny streets wind their way toward Christ Church. Meanwhile, the gentle incline of Dame Street, lined with Victorian buildings, descends toward the castle.

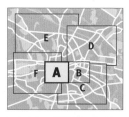

LEO BURDOCKS

THE LORD EDWARD

RESTAURANTS

The Bite of Life (**A** D3)
→ 55 Patrick's St
Tel. 454 2949
Mon-Fri 7.30am–4pm;
Sat 10am–4pm
A tiny café that makes sandwiches to order, to eat in or take out and, in summer, the adjacent park is a great place for a picnic. Jorinde Moynihan has a ready smile and a friendly greeting for her customers, which is a good enough reason itself to pay her a visit. Packed at lunchtimes. Salads, soup, sandwiches, and fresh juices (apple, ginger and carrot, etc.). €3–5.

Leo Burdocks (**A** E2)
→ 2 Werburgh St
Tel. 454 0306
Daily noon–midnight
The best fish and chips in the city... the proof is the long queue spilling out onto the street. Haddock, cod, salmon or grilled gudgeon, all served with real fries and a choice of sauces. À la carte €7.

Govinda's (**A** F4)
→ 4 Aungier St
Tel. 475 0309
Mon-Sat noon–9pm
A small vegetarian restaurant run by Hare Krishna followers. A Zen atmosphere permeates

the spicy soups, spring rolls and fried cheeses.
Main course €9.

Gruel (**A** F2)
→ 68a Dame St
Tel. 670 1719
Daily noon–10pm (9pm Sun)
Imagine an American diner crossed with a classic French bistro or a local deli crossed with an arty museum café and you have Gruel, a hugely successful and fashionable eating-house. The decor features tiled floors, posters, globe lampshades and pretty pink stools, while on the menu are sandwiches of all kinds, fresh cod fillets, tagines, and cakes to die for. À la carte €10–15.

Mermaid Café (**A** F2)
→ 69-70 Dame St
Tel. 670 8236 Mon-Sat
12.30-2.30pm, 6–11pm;
Sun 12.30-3.30pm, 6–9pm
Jazz and candlelight in an atmosphere of maritime New England. Impeccable service and elegant fare: risottos, gratins, skate with saffron, caramelized sweetbreads. Try the house specialty – the succulent crab cakes.
À la carte €30–35.

The Lord Edward (**A** E2)
→ 23 Christchurch Place
Tel. 454 2158
Mon-Fri 12.30–2.30pm,

RTERHOUSE THE BRAZEN HEAD WHICHCRAFT

6–10.15pm; Sat 6–10.15pm
On the top floor of a
tavern (1875), a luscious
19th-century dining room
serving fish dishes,
unrivaled elsewhere.
Sole in white wine, and
seafood and shrimp with
cucumber are among the
most popular dishes.
For dessert, meringue
drizzled with *crème
anglaise*. Main course
€25; à la carte €50.

TEAROOM, CAFÉ

Queen of Tarts (**A** E2)
→ *4 Cork Hill*
Tel. 670 7499
Mon-Fri 7.30am–6pm;
Sat 9.30am– 6pm;
Sun 10am–6pm
Relaxed, colorful tearoom
serving delicious savory
pastries (tomato, chicken,
spinach) and melt-in-the-
mouth cakes (crumbles,
muffins, plum puddings).
Bar Italia (**A** E2)
→ *Exchange St Lower*
Tel. 679 5128 Mon-Fri 8am–
8pm; Sat 9.30am–5pm
The paved terrace is the
ideal setting to taste the
best cappuccino in the
city. Crusty paninis
(sandwiches), from the
simplest to the highly
imaginative, all prepared
by Italian chefs. The
owners have also opened

Dunne & Crescenzi (**B** D3).

PUBS, CONCERTS

The Porterhouse (**A** F2)
→ *16-18 Parliament St*
Tel. 679 8847
Daily 11.30am–11.30pm
(1.30am Thu & Sun;
2am Fri; 2.30am Sat)
Stouts, bitters and lagers
– there are ten home-
brewed house beers
served straight from the
casks. Rows of bottles
are stacked on the four
floors, which groan under
the weight of it all. Live
music every day, with
traditional music on Sun.
One of the best pubs in
Dublin – don't miss.
The Brazen Head (**A** C1)
→ *20 Bridge St Lower*
Tel. 679 5186
Mon-Sat 10.30am–midnight;
(12.30am Fri-Sat);
Sun noon–midnight
The oldest pub in Dublin
– the year 1198 is proudly
on display across the
walls, ceiling and even
the floor. Irish, blues and
country music every night .
O'Shea Merchant (**A** C1)
→ *12 Bridge St Lower*
Tel. 679 6793
Daily 10.30am–1am
There are few tables here,
so you'll probably end up
leaning at the bar for your
Guinness. In the evenings

dancers take over the
white wooden dance floor.
Irish music, naturally.
Olympia Theatre (**A** F2)
→ *72 Dame St*
Tel. 679 3323 Concerts 8pm
(depending on program)
Seating for 1,300 people
in this Victorian theater
with a varied program of
acts. David Bowie or
The Divine Comedy
alternate with operettas,
theater pieces and
music-hall acts.
Vicar Street (**A** A2)
→ *58-59 Thomas St*
Tel. 454 6656
Daily 8pm–12.30am
(varies according to
program)
A concert hall that can
accommodate up to
1,000 dancers or drinkers
seated at funny little
tables in the shape of
numbers. The place also
stages comedy shows.
The Front Lounge (**A** F2)
→ *33 Parliament St*
Tel. 670 4112
Mon-Fri noon–11.30pm
(2.30am Fri); Sat 2pm-
2.30am; Sun 2–11.30pm
A comfortable lounge and
bar mainly patronized by
the gay community. At
weekends a DJ drives the
place wild with electro-
funk music. Quiet in the
early evenings, but
packed solid at weekends.

SHOPPING

Whichcraft (**A** E2)
→ *Cow's Lane / 30 Castle St*
Tel. 474 1011 / 679 3775
Mon-Fri 9.30am–6.30pm
(8pm Thu); Sat 9am-
6.30pm; Sun 10am– 6pm
Rocking chairs, jewelry,
ceramics and various
objects all straight out of a
fairytale. This shop has a
comprehensive range of
modern Irish craftwork.
The Irish Historical
Picture Company (**A** F1)
→ *5 Ormond Quay Lower*
Tel. 872 0144
Daily 9am– 6pm
(5pm Sat-Sun)
Hundreds of prints and
old photographs depicting
scenes of Dublin life and
the city's history. A shrine
to the world of images…
and to antique hunting.
Francis Street (**A** C3)
The main street for
antique stores.
Design associate
→ *no. 144-145*
Tel. 453 7795
Tue-Sun 10.30am–5pm
Retro furniture and
furnishing fabrics.
Esther Sexton Antiques
→ *no. 51. Tel. 473 0909*
Mon-Sat 10am–5pm
This shop sells
magnificent mirrors and
splendid Victorian and
Edwardian style furniture.

ST AUDOEN'S

DUBLINIA

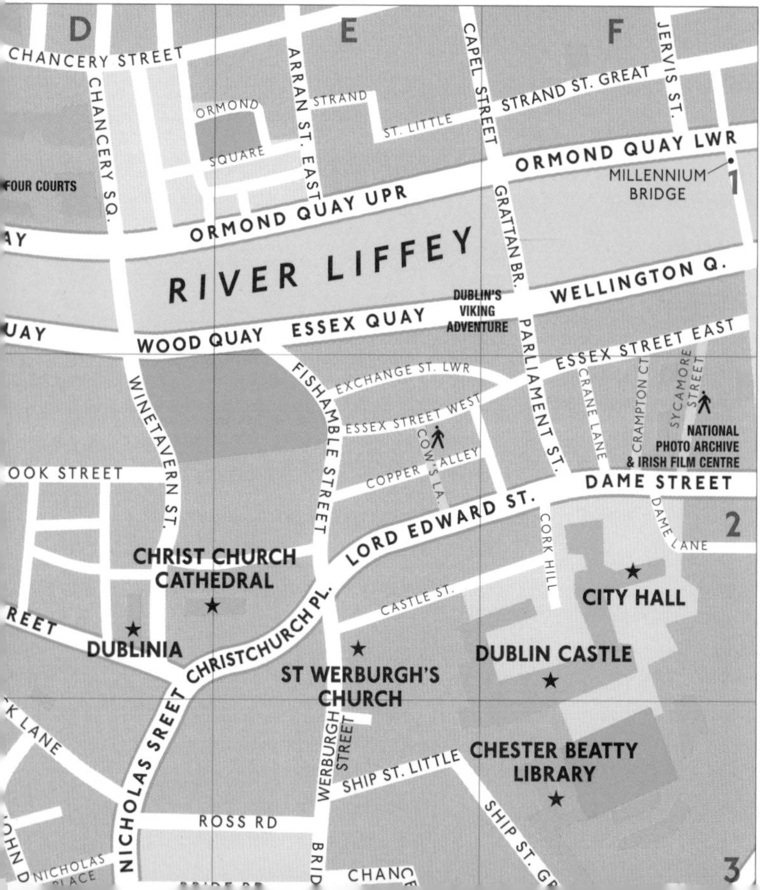

Map

CHANCERY STREET

CHANCERY SQ.

FOUR COURTS

ORMOND SQUARE

ORMOND ST. EAST

ARRAN ST. EAST

STRAND ST. LITTLE

STRAND STRAND ST. GREAT

CAPEL STREET

JERVIS ST.

ORMOND QUAY LWR

MILLENNIUM BRIDGE

D **E** **F**

ORMOND QUAY UPR

QUAY

RIVER LIFFEY

GRATTAN BR.

WELLINGTON Q.

WOOD QUAY ESSEX QUAY

DUBLIN'S VIKING ADVENTURE

ESSEX STREET EAST

PARLIAMENT ST.

CRANE LANE

CRAMPTON CT.

SYCAMORE STREET

EXCHANGE ST. LWR

FISHAMBLE STREET

ESSEX STREET WEST

COW'S ALLEY

COPPER ALLEY

COPPER LA.

NATIONAL PHOTO ARCHIVE & IRISH FILM CENTRE

DAME STREET

WINETAVERN ST.

OOK STREET

LORD EDWARD ST.

CORK HILL

DAME LANE

2

CHRIST CHURCH CATHEDRAL
★

CASTLE ST.

★ **CITY HALL**

REET

DUBLINIA
★

CHRISTCHURCH PL.

ST WERBURGH'S CHURCH
★

DUBLIN CASTLE
★

NICHOLAS STREET

K LANE

WERBURGH STREET

SHIP ST. LITTLE

CHESTER BEATTY LIBRARY
★

SHIP ST. GR

→ Map B

OHN NICHOLAS PLACE

ROSS RD

BRIDE

CHANG

BRIDE RD

3

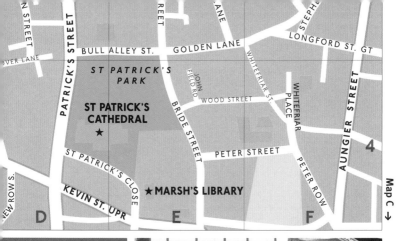

Map C →

CASTLE

CHESTER BEATTY LIBRARY

CITY HALL

...ia, a pretty covered ...e leads to Christ ...h.

...rist Church
...dral (A D2)
→ ...stchurch Place
...7 8099 Mon-Fri
...n–4.30pm; Sat 10am–
...; Sun 12.45–2.45pm
...e, Richard de Clare
...gbow') built a stone
...dral on the site of the
...r wooden church.
...then, Victorian neo-
...c renovations have
...mposed on the
...al Roman style, but
...perb capitals remain,
...with a 12th-century
...d crypt. Among the
...ed reclining figures, is
...f Strongbow himself,

in full armor. At one time, this statue was used as a table by unscrupulous traders.

★ St Werburgh's Church (A E2)
→ Werburgh St. Tel. 478 3710 (visits by appointment)
Fire and the 1798 revolt caused the castle parish church to lose its belltower. The elegant interior, restored in the 18th century, now boasts a baroque organ, tiled floor and dark-wood sculptures.

★ Dublin Castle (A F2)
→ Castle St. Tel. 677 7129 Mon-Fri 10am–4.45pm; Sat-Sun 2–4.45pm
This was the seat of English rule for 700 years. The

medieval building has almost totally disappeared – two towers and under-ground fortifications are all that remain. Above the bleak cellars is a series of sumptuous, brightly colored 18th-century rooms with stuccos, tapestries and inlaid woodwork. Also a dazzling ballroom with crystal chandeliers.

★ Chester Beatty Library (A F3)
→ Dublin Castle, Castle St Tel. 407 0750 Mon-Fri 10am–5pm (closed Mon Oct-April); Sat 11am–5pm; Sun 1–5pm
Irish-American mining magnate Sir Alfred Chester Beatty (1875–1968) spent his life gathering the most

extraordinary treasures, bequeathing them to the Irish people upon his death. Chinese silk paintings, Japanese woodblock prints, European medieval and Renaissance manuscripts, illuminated copies of the Koran and other exquisitely bound books.

★ City hall (A F2)
→ Dame St Mon-Sat 10am–5.15pm; Sun 2–5pm
Greek Revival (1769) seat of the royal stock exchange, then the city hall. Between the columns are statues of Irish heros dressed in togas! Stunning rotunda painted with frescos, with a rose window flickering at its center.

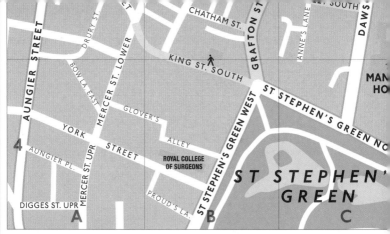

CHATHAM ST.

KING ST. SOUTH

ST STEPHEN'S GREEN WEST

ST STEPHEN'S GREEN NO

GRAFTON ST

ANNE'S LANE

DAWS

SOUTH

MAN
HO

AUNGIER STREET

DRURY ST.

BOWLA EAST

MERCER ST. LOWER

GLOVER'S

YORK STREET

ALLEY

4

AUNGIER PL.

MERCER ST. UPR

ROYAL COLLEGE
OF SURGEONS

ST STEPHEN'
GREEN

PROUD'S LA.

DIGGES ST. UPR

A

ST STEPHEN'S GREEN WEST

B

C

MANSION HOUSE

NATIONAL MUSEUM OF ARCHAEOLOGY

LEINSTER HOUSE

B

★ **Temple Bar** (**B** A-B1)
→ *Between Dame St and
the waterfront*
A maze of zigzagging little
streets which are thronged
with people day and night.
Following major redevelopment work in the 1990s, the
area is now packed with
movie theaters, shops,
cabaret venues and cultural
centers. In the heart of this
trendy district, Meeting
House Square stages
shows, concerts and open-
air movies in summer. There
is a vegetable fair every Sat.

★ **National Photographic
Archive** (**B** A1)
→ *Meeting House Square
Tel. 603 0200 Mon–Fri 10am–
5pm; Sat 10am–2pm*

This unique collection of
300,000 images is part of
the National Library of
Ireland, and consists of
photographs relating to the
country's history, cultural
and social life. The archive
is available for consultation,
and regular exhibitions
show a selection of the
collection's pictures –
'Dublin from the 1950s to
1970s', 'Irish Transportation
from 1937 to 1970', etc.

★ **Bank of Ireland /
Arts Centre** (**B** B2)
→ *Bank of Ireland: 2 College
Green. Tel. 671 2261
Guided tours of the Lords'
Chamber: Tue 10.30am,
11.30am and 1.45pm.
Arts Centre: Foster Place*

*Tel. 671 2261 Guided tours at
10am, 11am and 3pm*
This massive, windowless
parliament building became
a bank in 1803, after the
Union of Great Britain and
Ireland. Don't miss the gold-
coffered ceiling and the
enormous 18th-century
tapestries depicting the
impressive figure of William
of Orange at the Battle of
the Boyne (1690). Two
hundred years of the bank's
history can be seen on
video at the arts center,
along with an exhibition of
coins and banknotes (1690).

★ **Trinity College** (**B** D1)
→ *College Green
Tel. 608 2320 Old Library:
daily 9.30am–4.30pm;*

Oct–April: Mon–Sat 9.30
5pm; Sun noon–4.30pm
Founded by Elizabeth
the pride of the city, th
perfect copy of an Oxf
style college. Oscar W
Samuel Beckett and E
Stoker were once stud
here. At the entrance,
angels of the belltowe
overlook the *Rubrics* (
quarters dating back
years). In the Old Libr
the Long Room archiv
copies of every book
published in the Britis
since 1801. The Treasu
contains the illuminat
manuscripts of the 8th
century *Book of Kells*,
world's most unique C
treasure. Each piece c

↑ Map E

TEMPLE BAR

NATIONAL PHOTOGRAPHIC ARCHIVE

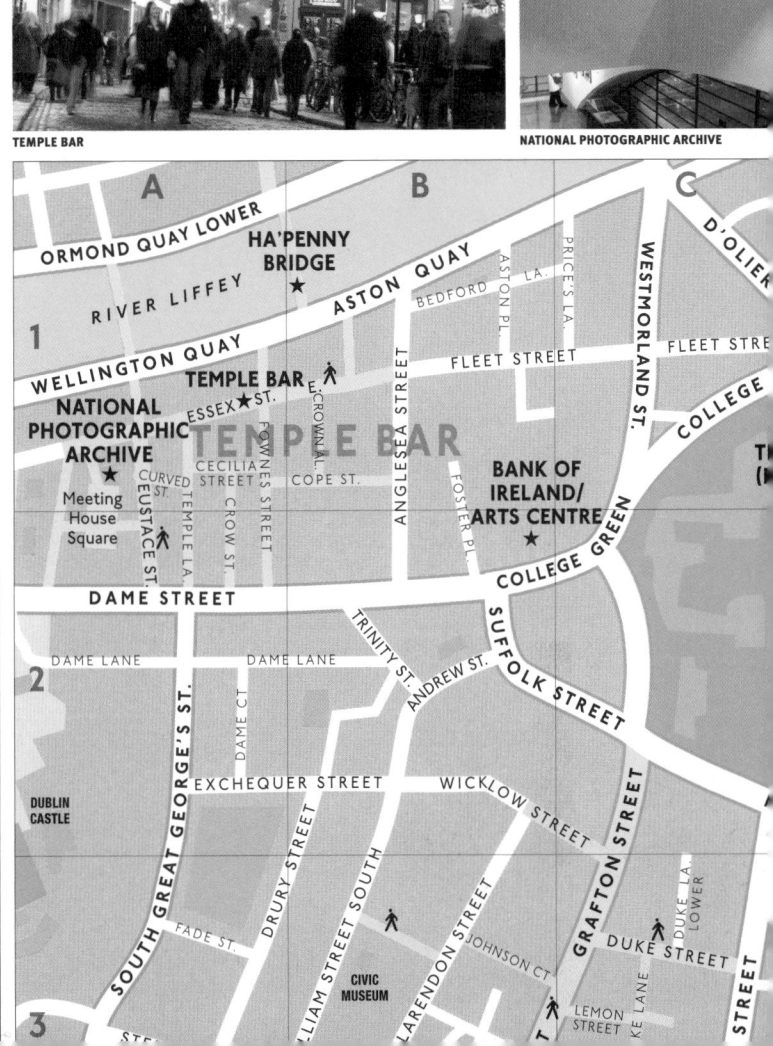

	A	B	C

ORMOND QUAY LOWER

HA'PENNY BRIDGE ★

RIVER LIFFEY

ASTON QUAY

D'OLIER

1

WELLINGTON QUAY

BEDFORD

ASTON PL.

PRICE'S LA.

WESTMORLAND ST.

FLEET STREET

FLEET STRE

TEMPLE BAR 🚶

ANGLESEA STREET

COLLEGE

NATIONAL PHOTOGRAPHIC ARCHIVE ★

ESSEX ★ ST.

E.CROWN AL.

TEMPLE BAR

T (

Meeting House Square ★

CURVED ST.

EUSTACE ST.

TEMPLE LA.

FOWNES STREET

CECILIA STREET

CROW ST.

COPE ST.

FOSTER PL.

BANK OF IRELAND/ ARTS CENTRE ★

DAME STREET

COLLEGE GREEN

2

DAME LANE

DAME LANE

TRINITY ST.

SUFFOLK STREET

DAME CT.

ANDREW ST.

DUBLIN CASTLE

EXCHEQUER STREET

WICKLOW STREET

GRAFTON STREET

SOUTH GREAT GEORGE'S ST.

DRURY STREET

WILLIAM STREET SOUTH

CLARENDON STREET

DUKE STREET

DUKE LA. LOWER

🚶

FADE ST.

JOHNSON CT.

KE LANE

LEMON STREET

3

CIVIC MUSEUM

STREET

Nowhere in Dublin is there a more lively atmosphere than on the pedestrianized sidewalks of this area, from the chic stores of Grafton Street to the busy Temple Bar area. Shopping and cultural activities can be followed up with a night out in one of the various bars and clubs. The superb Trinity College and the Bank loom over the passers-by: one a symbol of learning, the other of economic order. One curved street, prettily bordered by College Green, runs toward Kildare Street (the museum district), where magnificent former townhouses now contain some of Ireland's national treasures.

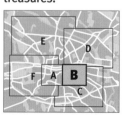

DUNNE & CRESCENZI

SIXTY6

RESTAURANTS

Simon's Place (B A2)
→ 22 South Great George's St .Tel. 679 7821
Mon-Sat 8.30am–5pm
A hospitable atmosphere redolent with the aroma of cappuccino, and friendly service. Host Simon spares no effort to put his broad mix of clients at their ease. Sandwiches, delicious soups and cinnamon doughnuts.
À la carte €5–10.

Dunne & Crescenzi (B D3)
→ 14/16 South Frederick St
Tel. 677 3815
Mon-Sat 8.30am–11pm;
Sun noon–11pm
Try some Italian antipasti washed down with a glass of wine, served in a pleasant Italian ambience.
À la carte €10.

The Bad Ass Café (B B1)
→ 9/11 Crown Alley
Tel. 671 2596 Daily 11.30am–10pm (11pm Thu-Sun)
A lively cafeteria frequented by students, professionals and workers alike. Pizzas, pasta or ice cream, orders fly through the air on an ingenious pulley system. À la carte €15–20.

The Mongolian Barbeque (B B1)
→ 7 Anglesea St

Tel. 670 4154 Mon-Fri 3.30–11pm; Sat-Sun 12.30–11pm
Mongolian fare in Temple Bar. Fill your bowl with you choice of meat and vegetables and then hand it to the expert chef for it to be stir fried on a hotplate.
À la carte €15–35.

Sixty6 (B A2)
→ 66-67 South Great George's St. Tel. 400 5878
Daily 8am–10pm
Chic bohemian brasserie with pictures by local artists on the walls, friendly waiters in long aprons. The menu features such delicacies as swordfish with capers, lamb steak with rosemary, and brasserie classics at reasonable prices. À la carte €25–35.

CAFÉ

Bewleys Café (B B3)
→ 78-79 Grafton St
Tel. 672 7720
Mon-Sat 8am–1am;
Sun 9am–11pm
A fashionable spot, and a place with something to offer all throughout the day. People come here to enjoy an early breakfast, to dine, or simply to relax ove a coffee. In the afternoons and evenings the café plays host to comedy acts, concerts or dance shows.

ERNATIONAL BAR   RI-RA   BROWN THOMAS

CULTURAL CENTERS

The Irish Film Institute (B A2)
→ 6 Eustace St
Tel. 679 5744 Mon-Sat 10am–12.30am (1.30am Thu; 2.30am Fri-Sat); Sun 1–3pm.
www.irishfilm.ie
This splendid Quaker house, dating from the 17th century, is dedicated to international art house cinema. Retrospectives and festivals.

Project Arts Centre (B A1)
→ 39 Essex St East
Tel. 881 9613/14 Mon-Sat 10–7pm, show at 8pm.
www.project.ie
This minimalist building painted a cold shade of blue houses Dublin's temple to alternative arts: dance, plays, poetry.

PUBS, CLUBS

Grogan's (B B3)
→ 15 William St South
Tel. 677 9320 Mon-Sat 10.30am–11.30pm (12.30am Fri-Sat); Sun 12.30–11pm
A classic Irish bar 'where time stands still', as the saying goes – and Grogan's has even printed this motto on its menu. Attractive posters on the walls and friendly bar staff make this one of the most

relaxing places in town. At weekends it's so full you can hardly get to the bar.

The International Bar (B B2)
→ 23 Wicklow St
Tel. 677 9250 Mon-Sat 10.30am–11.30pm (12.30am Thu-Sat); Sun 11.30am–11pm
A sports bar by day, this venue hosts free events at night: jazz, blues, one-man shows or Irish dancing.

Oliver John Gogarty (B B1)
→ 58-59 Fleet St
Tél. 671 1822 Daily 10.30am–2.30am (1am Sun)
Farm-style interior with cartwheels and barrels, furious music until 2am and tasty all-day Irish breakfasts. Touristy but worth a visit.

Kehoe's (B C3)
→ 9 Anne St South
Tel. 677 8312
Daily 10.30am–11.30pm, (12.30am Fri-Sat; 11pm Sun)
Students, businessmen and people from all walks of life flock to this 200-year-old city pub. Quiet in the daytimes but very busy in the evening at weekends, when there's enough Guinness downed here to float a battleship.

Temple Bar Music Center (B A1)
→ Curved St
Tel. 670 9202 Concerts at

8–9pm, late sessions at 11pm (according to program)
A Dublin institution, featuring live music of all kinds, from reggae to rock and rap, with great electro sessions featuring sounds from such labels as DeeJay Gigolos and B-Pitch Control International.

Ri-Ra (B A2)
→ Dame Court (or entrance on South Great George's St)
Tel. 671 1220 Daily 11pm (10.30am Sat-Sun)– 2.30am
This busy nightspot is located below the Globe bar, which has the same owner. The music is extremely eclectic and includes house, hip-hop, Latino, with occasional nostalgic forays back to the 1970s and 80s.

SHOPPING

Urban Outfitters (B A1)
→ Cecilia St / Fownes St
Tel. 670 6202 Mon-Sat 10am–8pm (7pm Fri-Sat); Sun noon–6pm
Gadgets and fashionable ready-to-wear in a stunning building. A good place to keep up with Irish trends.

Avoca (B B2)
→ 11-13 Suffolk St
Tel. 677 4215
Mon-Sat 10am–6pm (8pm Thu); Sun 11am–6pm

A resolutely Irish department store with character, selling toys, household linens, home- and kitchenware. Fantastic display of scones and muffins in the fine foods department downstairs.

Grafton St (B B3-C2)
One of Dublin's most commercial streets.

Brown Thomas
→ Tel. 605 6666 Mon-Sat 9am–8pm (9pm Thu; 7pm Sat); Sun 10am–7pm
Luxury clothing and haute couture for men and women. Ultra chic.

Dunnes Stores
→ Tel. 671 4629
Mon-Thu, Sat (am–6.30pm; Fri and Sun noon–6pm
The Irish Marks and Spencer.

St Stephen's Green Centre
→ Tel. 478 0888
Mon-Sat 9am–6pm (9pm Thu); Sun and public hols noon–6pm
Smart department store selling perfumes, designer clothing, etc.

George's St Arcade (B A2)
→ South Great George's St
Mon-Sat 9am–5pm
A 19th-century redbrick shopping gallery with second-hand stores selling books, records, clothes and memorabilia, and several cafés as well.

HNY BRIDGE

BANK OF IRELAND

TRINITY COLLEGE

LBEG
EET

D

TARA STREET

LUKE STREET

TARA STREET
STATION

E

MOSS STREET

GLOUCESTER

RATH ROW

BRACKEN'S
LANE

PRINCES ST. SOUTH

ST. S.

F

CITY Q.

PETERSON'S
COURT

TOWNSEND STREET

TOWNSEND ST.

DAWLING'S
COURT

1

LLEGE
ELLS)

PEARSE STREET

CARDS
LANE

SPRING GDN LA

SHAW STREET

MARK STREET

MARK'S LANE

LOMBARD ST. EAST

PARK LANE EAST

PEARSE STREET

MAGENNIS
PLACE

COLLEGE
PARK

PEARSE
STATION

2

↑ Map C

DENTAL HOSPITAL

COLLEGE LANE

WESTLAND ROW

CUMBERLAND ST. SOUTH

REET

SOUTH

LEINSTER ST.

LINCOLN PL.

FREDERICK LA. S.

E STREET

LEINSTER LA

HERALDIC
MUSEUM

CLARE

LA

ERRIOW

T LWR

FENIAN ST.

3

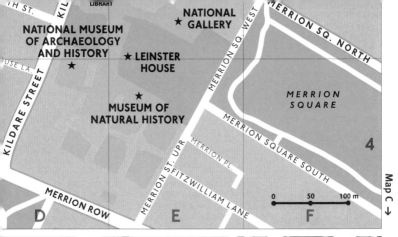

TH ST. · KIL · LIBRARY

NATIONAL MUSEUM OF ARCHAEOLOGY AND HISTORY

NATIONAL GALLERY

MERRION SQ. WEST · MERRION SQ. NORTH

★ LEINSTER HOUSE

MERRION SQUARE

MUSEUM OF NATURAL HISTORY

KILDARE STREET · USE LA. · OUSE LA.

MERRION ST. UPR · MERRION SQUARE SOUTH

MERRION PL. · FITZWILLIAM LANE

MERRION ROW

4

Map C →

0   50   100 m

D   E   F

NATIONAL GALLERY

MUSEUM OF NATURAL HISTORY

is made of half a hide, with semi-us stones to color the ng: lazurite or hite.

penny Bridge (B B1) 919 there was a half-toll (hence the nick-to cross Wellington , a footbridge arching ully across the Liffey.

nsion House (B C4) son St ding his baroque , Joshua Dawson d what was to be one main stages for d's nationalist ment. In 1919, the r the declaration of endence took place in on. Today, it is the

official home of Dublin's Lord Mayor.

★ **National Museum of Archaeology and History (B** D4)

→ Kildare St. Tel. 677 7444 Tue-Sat 10am–5pm; Sun 2–5pm. www.museum.ie This neoclassical palace by Thomas Deane is a very worthy setting for Ireland's antiquities, a unique collection of items dating from the Iron Age through to the 18th century. Don't miss the prehistoric gold jewelry (the finest collection of its kind in Europe), especially the stunning Ardagh Chalice and Tara Brooch (both 8th century). The journey through time ends with the

war of independence: touching photographs and film footage of the riots.

★ **Leinster House (B** E3) → Kildare St. Tel. 618 3000 Visits by appointment Built in 1745 by the architect Cassels, this building is said to have served as the model for the White House. Today, it is the seat of Parliament. The façade has not changed since the Duke of Leinster resided here.

★ **National Gallery (B** E3) → Merrion Square West Tel. 661 5133 Mon-Sat 9.30am–5.30pm (8.30pm Thu); Sun noon–5.30pm. www.nationalgallery.ie Built 150 years ago, this museum houses an

impressive collection of paintings – Irish works alongside Italian, Spanish, Dutch, Flemish, English and French. Also, portraits of Yeats' family and some unusual sculptures, including a very lifelike one of the writer G.B. Shaw.

★ **Museum of Natural History (B** E4)

→ Merrion Square West Tel. 677 7444 Tue-Sat 10am–5pm; Sun 2–5pm. www.museum.ie Insects, elephants, sharks marmots... an infinite number of species are now housed in this Victorian manor house. There are also three 10,000 year-old elk skeletons.

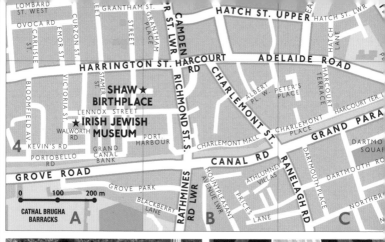

MERRION SQUARE

NUMBER 29

★ Carmelite Church (C A2)
→ *56 Aungier St. Tel. 475 8821 Daily 7.45am–6pm (9.15pm Tue; 730pm Sat-Sun). Public holidays 9.30am–1pm*
This warm 19th-century church, attributed to Papworth, replaced a 1539 priory. It provided a cozy refuge for *Our Lady of Dublin*, the only madonna to survive the ransacking of the Reformation. It is also a lovely setting for the effigy and relics of the Roman martyr St Valentine.

★ Royal College of Surgeons (C B2)
→ *St Stephen's Green*
Rounded steps, arched windows and Doric columns, the Royal College of Surgeons (1806), one of the loveliest buildings around St Stephen's, is also the one that has sustained the most damage. In 1916, during the Easter Rising, it withstood British assault against Irish nationalists. The building was not completely destroyed but bullet holes in the columns are still visible today.

★ St Stephen's Green (C C2)
→ *Daily 730am (9.30am Sun) until sunset*
This 22-acre park was made possible by the generosity of Arthur Guinness. Its cheery lawns, winding leafy paths, duck pond, weeping willows and kiosks provide a haven for strollers and school children alike. Visit the avenue of busts of poets such as Yeats, Joyce and Markievicz and don't miss the monument to the illustrious patriot Wolfe Tone (1763–98) at the north entrance. To the south is a touching memorial to children who died in the Great Famine of 1846.

★ Newman House (C B3)
→ *85-86 St Stephen's Green Tel. 475 7255 Guided tours June-Aug: Tue-Fri noon–5pm*
In two connected 18th-century townhouses, this Catholic university was founded by Cardinal Newman in 1865. The style is mixed with Ge in the remarkable stu ceilings by the Franci Brothers, and in scul of the Apollo room, w two nudes, considere indecent, were repair by the Jesuits.

★ Iveagh Gardens (
→ *Clonmel St. Tel. 475 Daily 8am (10am Sun)– (5pm Feb & Nov; 4pm D* Iveagh House, built in by Richard Castle, wa owned by the Guinne family. The elegant ga (waterfall, Venus foun magnificent rose gard and grottos) are an id

C

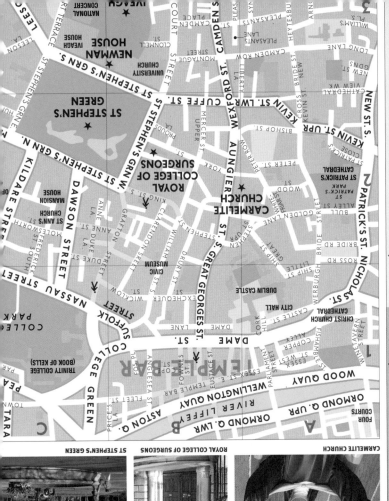

↓ Map E

CARMELITE CHURCH

ROYAL COLLEGE OF SURGEONS

ST STEPHEN'S GREEN

The magnificent parks of St Stephen and Merrion Square once formed part of the most fashionable district in Dublin. Beautiful 18th-century residences line the sloping streets leading down to the Grand Canal. Their ivy-covered red-brick walls and wrought-iron arches are particularly eye-catching. To the east, the docks and warehouses are closer than you think. To the west, businesses and cosmopolitan cafés stretch toward the south onto Wexford, Camden and Richmond streets.

BANG CAFÉ

BROWNE'S

RESTAURANTS

Havana Tapas bar (C B3)
→ 3 Camden St
Tel. 476 0046
Mon-Fri 11.30am–10.30pm (11.30pm Fri); Sat 1–11.30pm
Tapas bar watched over by a curious statue of St Domingo. Enjoy a glass of Rioja to latin rhythms. Great choice of delicious tapas (tortilla, fried chorizo, potato grilled with cheese), Spanish wine and sangria. Tapas €6.

Tulsi Indian (C D3)
→ 17a Baggot St Lower
Tel. 676 4578
Mon-Sat noon–2.30pm, 6–11.30pm; Sun 5–11pm
Excellent neighborhood's restaurant, where lamb, chicken, shrimp and vegetables are on offer with an infinite range of sauces. À la carte €15.

Bang Café (C C2)
→ 11 Merrion Row
Tel. 676 0898 Mon-Sat 12.30–3pm, 6–11pm
A light, minimalist setting for top quality Eurasian cuisine. Turbot with chanterelles mushrooms, saffron tartelettes, stewed cherries cooked in kirsch. À la carte €20–30.

Browne's (C C2)
→ 22 St Stephen's Green North. Tel. 638 3939 Daily 12.30–2.30pm, 6.30– 10pm (closed Sat lunch & Sun eve)
The high-class restaurant of the elegant Browne's Hotel, with parquet floors, snow-white napiery and crimson velvet recalling la belle époque in 19th-century Paris. Against a discreet background of jazz music, this is the place to feast on roast guinea-fowl, lobster or first-class smoked salmon. À la carte €60.

L'Ecrivain (C D3)
→ 109a Baggot St Lower
Tel. 661 1919
Mon-Fri 12.30–2pm, 7–10.30pm; Sat 7–10.30pm
The feather-shaped door handle hints at the delicate design of the interior of this restaurant, with bookcases and portraits of writers. Under the soft lighting, savor a no less delicate cuisine: monkfish, pheasant with apricots and fresh scallops. À la carte €75.

CAFÉ

Café Java (C D4)
→ 145 Leeson St Upper
Tel. 660 0675
Mon-Sat 7am (9am Sat)–4pm; Sun 10am–4pm
Stop here for breakfasts of all kinds – from the healthy, energizing ones (vegetarian dishes, bagels

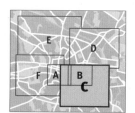

OBELLO

WHELAN'S

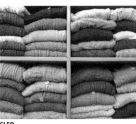
CLEO

porridge) to the truly full-fat ones (eggs, muffins, bacon, sausages). €5–10.

PUBS, CONCERTS, CLUBS

O'Donoghue (C C2)
→ 15 Merrion Row
Tel. 676 2807 Daily
10.30am–11.30pm (11pm
Sun; 12.30am Thu-Sat)
A world record was set here: the largest single order of drinks (400 pints). Each evening Irish music sets off a wave of frenzy – the photos on the walls prove it.

Portobello (C B4)
→ 33 Richmond St South
Tel. 475 2715
Mon-Sat 10.30am–2am;
Sun 5pm–2am
Opened in 1793 for canal workers to come and quench their thirst – those same canals which the neighborhood is so proud of today. Vast room filled with nooks in which you can eat lunch or listen to the DJs who play here every night.

The National Concert Hall (C C3)
→ Earlsfort Terrace
Tel. 417 0000 (box office)
Concerts at 8pm (varies according to program).
www.nch.ie
This red and gold building,

opened in 1865 by Queen Victoria, became, in 1981, a principal venue for the most illustrious classical orchestras, jazz bands and pop groups. The huge auditorium, with a four-keyboard organ, seats 1,200. In the more intimate John Field Room is a crystal chandelier with 14,564 pendants.

Whelan's (C B3)
→ 25 Wexford St.
Tel. 478 0766
Daily noon–3am (2am Sun)
Rock and folk concerts alternate with a nightclub in this tiny theater space next to a pub.

Carnival (C B3)
→ 11 Wexford St.
Tel. 405 3604 Mon-Sat
noon–midnight (Fri-Sat
1am); Sun 4pm–midnight
The sound of indie rock bounces off the walls of this sophisticated, dimly lit underground bar, popular with lovers of the latest sounds around, and jammed solid at weekends.

The Village (C B3)
→ 26 Wexford St
Tel. 475 8555
Mon-Fri 11am–2.30am;
Sat-Sun 5pm-2.30am
A great music venue underneath the street-level lounge featuring live concerts and events of all

kinds, together with local and international DJs: eclecticism is the keyword at The Village. Admission free before 10pm.

Pod/Redbox/ Lobby Bar (C B3)
→ Old Harcourt Station,
Harcourt St. Tel. 478 0225
Mon-Sat 5pm–12.30am
(2.30am Fri-Sat)
The Pod and the Redbox are two clubs playing a mixture of house and R'n'B in an old station. Meanwhile, the fashionable Lobby Bar will quench your thirst with some unusual cocktails.

SHOPPING

Louise Kennedy (C D2)
→ 56 Merrion Square
Tel. 662 0056 Mon-Sat 9am
(9.30am Sat)–6pm
Louise Kennedy, a designer with an excellent reputation, artistically displays her creations in her own house. Hats, scarves, and assorted gloves, vases and statuettes.

Cleo (C C2)
→ 18 Kildare St. Tel. 676 1421
Mon-Sat 9am–5.30pm
Authentic traditional sweaters and tweed suits from all over Ireland. Each piece is unique, so prices are high.

The Celtic Whiskey Shop (C C2)
→ 27-28 Dawson St
Tel. 675 9744 Mon-Sat
10.30am–8pm (9pm Thu-
Sat); Sun 12.30–6pm
The widest selection of whiskeys in Ireland, and the greatest variety of Irish whiskeys in the world. Among the most popular brands are Connemara and Redbreast. Tasting is available.

Louis Mulcahy (C C2)
→ 46 Dawson St
Tel. 670 9311 Mon-Sat
10am–6pm (8pm Thu)
Impeccably tasteful store selling pottery (pots, vases, teapots, cheese dishes) and amazing blue-green or golden-colored quilts.

The House of Ireland (C C1)
→ 37 Nassau St. Tel. 671 1111
Daily 9am–6pm (Wed 8pm)
A well-known store offering excellent value in tweeds, knitwear, de luxe crystal, porcelain and jewelry.

Bretzel Bakery (C B4)
→ 1 Lennox St. Tel. 475 2724
Mon-Fri 8.30am–6pm
(3pm Mon); Sat 9am–5pm;
Sun 9am–1pm
This tiny Jewish bakery first opened its doors in 1870. It sells bread and tomato foccacia baked in a wood oven, pretzels and traditional Jewish pastries.

AN HOUSE

IVEAGH GARDENS

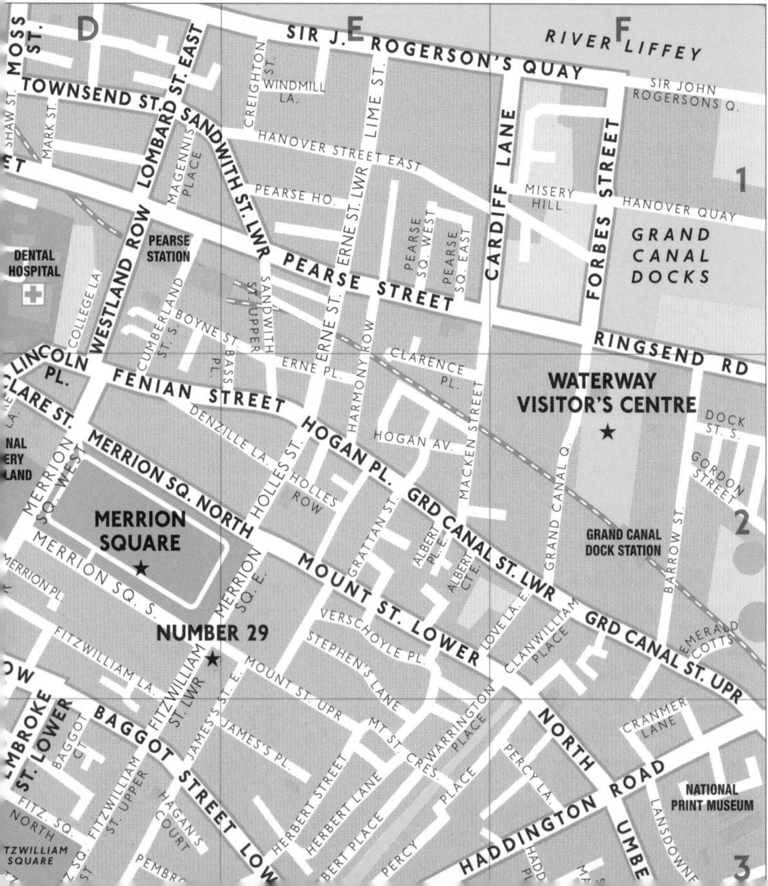

D

MOSS ST.

SHAW ST.

TOWNSEND ST.

MARK ST.

LOMBARD ST. EAST

SANDWITH ST. EAST

CREIGHTON ST.

WINDMILL LA.

SIR J. E ROGERSON'S QUAY

CREIGHTON ST.

LIME ST.

RIVER F LIFFEY

SIR JOHN ROGERSONS Q.

HANOVER STREET EAST

PEARSE HO.

DENTAL HOSPITAL

COLLEGE LA.

WESTLAND ROW

PEARSE STATION

MAGENNIS PLACE

CUMBERLAND ST. LWR

SANDWITH ST. LWR

BOYNE ST.

SANDWITH ST. UPPER

PEARSE STREET

ERNE ST. LWR

PEARSE SQ. WEST

PEARSE SQ. EAST

CARDIFF LANE

FORBES STREET

MISERY HILL

HANOVER QUAY

1

GRAND CANAL DOCKS

RINGSEND RD

LINCOLN PL.

CLARE ST.

FENIAN STREET

CUMBERLAND ST. BASS PL.

ERNE PL.

HARMONY ROW

CLARENCE PL.

WATERWAY VISITOR'S CENTRE ★

DOCK ST. S.

NAL ERY LAND

MERRION SQ. WEST

MERRION SQ. NORTH

DENZILLE LA.

HOLLES ST.

HOLLES ROW

HOGAN PL.

HOGAN AV.

GRD CANAL ST. LWR

MACKEN STREET

GRAND CANAL Q.

GRD CANAL ST. UPR

GRAND CANAL DOCK STATION

GORDON STREET

BARROW ST.

2

MERRION SQUARE ★

MERRION SQ. S.

MERRION PL.

GRATTAN ST.

ALBERT PL. E.

ALBERT CT. E.

MOUNT ST. LOWER

LOVELA E.

CLANWILLIAM PLACE

EMERALD SCOTTS

MERRION SQUARE

NUMBER 29 ★

FITZWILLIAM LA.

FITZWILLIAM ST. LWR

MOUNT ST. E.

MERRION SQ. E.

VERSCHOYLE PL.

STEPHEN'S LANE

NORTH

CRANMER LANE

ROW

MBROKE ST. LOWER

BAGGOT STREET LOW

BAGGOT ST.

FITZWILLIAM ST. UPPER

HAGAN'S COURT

JAMES ST. E.

JAMES'S PL.

MOUNT ST. UPR

MT. ST. CRES.

HERBERT STREET

HERBERT LANE

WARRINGTON PLACE

PERCY PLACE

PERCY LA.

HADDINGTON ROAD

LANSDOWNE

NATIONAL PRINT MUSEUM

3

FITZWILLIAM SQUARE

FITZ. SQ. NORTH

PEMBR

HERBERT PLACE

BERT PLACE

PERCY

HADD

UMBE

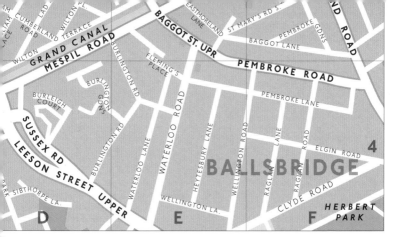

...WAY VISITOR'S CENTRE

SHAW BIRTHPLACE

IRISH JEWISH MUSEUM

to linger.

...rrion Square (C D2)

...wn–sunset

...ful square, striking for ...rfect architectural ...ony. In 1745, the arrival ... Count of Kildare at ...f the red-brick houses ... the Georgian square ...red an influx of high ...ty, and Merrion ...ne the most sought ...square in the city; ...es tell of the various ...rities who once lived ... A statue of Oscar ... even sprang up in the ...n opposite his own ...ence. Behind an ...e of dense trees, a ...e quiet reigns on the

central lawn – a popular spot for painters on Sundays.

★ **Number 29 (C** D2)

→ *Fitzwilliam St Lower Tel. 702 6165 Tue-Sat 10am–5pm; Sun 1–5pm*

A delightful residence (1794), that of Mrs Beatty, gives a fascinating insight into what was then a comfortable and bourgeois existence. From the dining room, kitchen, study to the bedrooms, nothing has changed since the early 19th century. Delft porcelain, four-poster bed with old-fashioned hot-water bottle, 1820s dolls' house, needlework...

★ **Waterway Visitor's Centre (C** F2)

→ *Grand Canal Quay Tel. 677 7510 June-Sep: daily 9.30am–5.30pm; Oct-May: Wed-Sun 12.30–5pm*

This fascinating museum is a glass cube floating in the middle of the canal among the warehouses. It tells you everything there is to know about canals (their history, the life of divers and dockers) using excellent slide shows.

★ **Shaw Birthplace (C** A4)

→ *33 Synge St. Tel 475 0854 May-Sep: Mon-Tue, Thu-Fri 10am–1pm, 2–5pm; Sat-Sun & public holidays 2–5pm*

Restored Victorian house,

birthplace of the famous playwright. See Shaw's nursery and the salon where his mother 'Speranza' once held literary evenings.

★ **Irish Jewish Museum (C** A4)

→ *3 Walworth Rd Tel. 490 1857 May-Sep: Tue-Thu, Sun 11am–3.30pm. Oct-April: Sun 10.30am–2.30pm*

This former synagogue is now a museum depicting the life of Dublin's small Jewish community. Photographs, kippas, candlesticks and tables laid out for sabbath. Upstairs is an astonishing life-like reconstruction of a Jewish wedding.

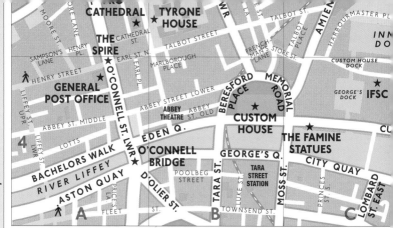

CUSTOM HOUSE

THE FAMINE STATUES

★ **O'Connell Bridge** (D A4)
Amazing four-lane bridge (1794), wider than it is long, leading toward the busy north district. At the end of the bridge is an enormous bronze statue of Daniel O'Connell himself (1775–1847), nicknamed 'The Liberator' by the Catholics. It watches over the avenue named after him, whose central reservation is lined with statues of historic figures.

★ **General Post Office (GPO)** (D A4)
→ O'Connell St. Tel. 705 7000 Mon–Sat 8am–8pm
The original post office was a neoclassical building by Johnson, the famous 18th-

century architect. During the Easter Rising of 1916, it was taken over by the nationalists, lead by poet Pearse, socialist Connolly and the fierce Countess Markievicz. Most of those involved were sentenced to death, and became martyrs to their cause. Rebuilt in 1929, the GPO's columns are still riddled with bullet holes.

★ **The Spire** (D A4)
→ O'Connell St
A tapering stainless steel mast over 360 ft high, right at the city center. Completed in January 2003, the Spire was constructed to herald the arrival of the 21st century and to celebrate the

complete refurbishment of O'Connell St. Its shiny surfaces reflect the colors of the sky: silver-grey in the daytime, it glows a mysterious, metallic blue at dawn and dusk. Its glittering peak provides a useful landmark all over the city.

★ **St Mary's Pro-Cathedral** (D A3)
→ 83 Marlborough St
Tel. 874 5441 Mon–Sat 7.30am–6.45pm (7.15pm Sat); Sun 9am–1.45pm, 5.30–7.45pm
Tall and dark, this is Dublin's only Catholic cathedral (1825). Inside, rose and silver tones dazzle, while, for services, the powerful organ resonates

with requiems, fugue toccatas.

★ **Tyrone House** (D
→ Marlborough St
Way ahead of its time (1740), the elegant residence of Sir Marcu Beresford (Count of Ty makes use of the clea that were to become s common in modern architecture. The taler Cassels and the Franc brothers blend perfec

★ **Custom House** (D
→ Custom House Quay Tel. 888 2538 Mon–Fri 12.30pm; Sat–Sun 2–5p Nov–mid March: Wed–Fri 10am–12.30pm; Sun 2– A tall, long, white arca building which runs a

D

MOUNTJOY SQUARE

GAA MUSEUM GAELIC ATHLETIC ASSOCIATION

CROKE PARK

ROTUNDA HOSPITAL

GATE THEATRE

GARDEN OF REMEMBRANCE

FINDLATERS CHURCH

JAMES JOYCE CENTRE

BELVEDERE HOUSE

PARNELL SQ. E.

SUMMERHILL

GARDINER ST. MID.

GARDINER ST. UPR.

DORSET ST.

N. CIRCULAR ROAD

ROYAL CANAL

CLONLIFFE ROAD

DRUMCONDRA ROAD LOWER

NORTH CIRCULAR ROAD

PORTLAND RD

SUMMERHILL PARADE

GARDINER ST.

PARNELL ST.

CONNOLLY STATION

DRUMCONDRA STATION

INNISFALLEN PAR.

ECCLES PLACE

LEO STREET

SYNNOTT PL.

FITZROY AVENUE

RUSSELL AVENUE

ELIZABETH ST.

JONES'S ROAD

ST IGNATIUS ROAD

WHITWORTH ROAD

ST PATRICK'S RD

ST ANNE'S RD NORTH

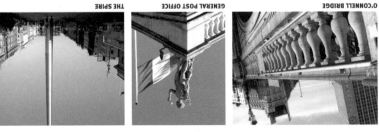

O'CONNELL BRIDGE

GENERAL POST OFFICE

THE SPIRE

Along the north bank are many attractive little parts of town waiting to be discovered. O'Connell Street, dominated by the Spire, a tall, stainless steel spike, is the largest thoroughfare in the city, and its sidewalks are lined with fast-food outlets, garish neon window displays and other commercial buildings hastily constructed alongside memorials to the wars of independence. Between Talbot and Henry streets is a great place to pick up a bargain in any one of many cut-price stores. At the heart of the former docks is the IFSC, the nerve center of high finance in Ireland whose empire is gradually spreading along the banks of the Liffey.

101 TALBOT STREET

CAFÉ SORRENTO

RESTAURANTS

Beshoff (D A4)
→ 7 O'Connell St Upper
Tel. 872 4400
Daily noon–10pm
Quality fish and chips in a restaurant with a simple and modern decor and large bay windows. The perfect setting to sample a local specialty. Menu €6.50.

Sheries (D B4)
→ 3 Abbey St Lower
Tel. 874 7237
Mon–Sat 8am–8pm
An Irish restaurant where you can get breakfast until the early evening, before going on to catch a play at the Abbey Theater nearby. À la carte €10–15.

The Italian Connection (D B3)
→ 95 Talbot St
Tel. 878 7125 Mon–Sat 8am–10pm; Sun 10am–10pm
The pizzas here sell fast and furious, thanks largely to the restaurant's location between O'Connell St and the IFSC. Inside, the walls are decorated with murals of Tuscany and the Coliseum, and illuminated by candlelight after dark. Rapid service at lunchtimes, but more relaxed in the evenings. À la carte €10–20.

101 Talbot Street (D B3)
→ 100-102 Talbot St
Tel. 874 5011
Tue–Sat 5–11pm
A local favorite, with a friendly room looking out onto Talbot St. It's open for dinner or after-theater supper, and the food has a hint of the Mediterranean mixed into the Irish flavors: cod with parmesan, pasta with bacon and quite a few dishes for vegetarians too. Recommended.
À la carte €20–30.

D-One (D D4)
→ IFSC, Custom House Quay
Tel. 856 1622
Mon–Sat noon–3pm, 5–10pm; Sun noon–5pm
A high-tech restaurant in the financial district, serving fish and chips as well as chicken suprême to businessmen and women in a hurry. The minimalist decor reflects the design of the building, a simple glass cube standing right on the bank of the Liffey. As you might imagine, D-One, like the IFSC, is crowded during the week, but much quieter at weekends. Carte €20–40.

CAFÉ

Café Sorrento (D A4)
→ 74 Middle Abbey St
Tel. 872 9573 Mon–Fri 7am–

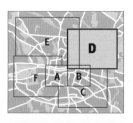

GAN'S   **EXCISE BAR**   **TALBOT STREET**

7pm; Sat 7.30am–6.30pm;
Sun 11am–6pm
Bright colors, fast service,
large salads, three-cheese
croissants – the perfect
place to stop before
climbing O'Connell and
Henry streets.

PUBS, THEATERS, CONCERTS

Harbourmaster (D C4)
→ IFSC, Custom House Dock
Tel. 670 1688
Sun–Thu 10am–11.30pm;
Fri 10am–12.30am;
Sat noon–12.30am;
Sun noon–11pm
Few tourists or old-timers
frequent this pavilion
overlooking the docks and
that's a shame. On a clear
day the terrace of the bar –
a favorite of IFSC workers
who come to drink a pint
or stop for a bite to eat
after work – has a relaxing
view over the calm waters.
The restaurant upstairs is
also very pleasant if you
get a table by the window.

Mulligan's (D B4)
→ 8 Poolberg St
Tel. 677 5582 Mon-Sat 11am–
11.30pm (12.30am Thu-Sat);
Sun 12.30–11pm
An authentic Irish pub
with three rooms in ruby
red, emerald green and
gold, in which to drink,
chat and pass the time.

The Celt Pub (D C3)
→ 81-82 Talbot St
Tel. 878 8655 Daily 10.30am–
11.30pm (12.30am Fri-Sat)
A quiet pub by day, rowdy
by night: the Irish jig starts
as soon as the clock
chimes 9.30pm.

Abbey Theatre/Peacock Theatre (D B4)
→ 26 Lower Abbey St
Tel. 878 7222 (box office)
www.abbeytheatre.ie
Founded in 1904 by Lady
Gregory and the poet
Yeats, the theater had its
fair share of setbacks
(riots and fires among
them) before attaining its
justified reputation. The
Abbey offers a classical
repertoire, the Peacock a
more contemporary one.

The Point (D F4)
→ North Wall Quay
Tel. 456 9569 (concerts from
8pm). www.thepoint.ie
This huge auditorium
(capacity 8,500), with the
look of a warehouse, is
located in a former
storehouse. Music and
dance of all kinds, from
opera to house, via
Riverdance.

Excise Bar (D D4)
→ IFSC, Mayor St Lower
Tel. 672 1873 Daily noon–
11.30pm (12.30am Fri-Sat)
Set on three levels in a
former warehouse, the
Excise is a restaurant by

day and a bar in the
evenings, and an
attractive fusion of old
and new.

The Vaults (D C3)
→ IFSC, Harbourmaster Place
Tel. 605 4700 Mon-Sat
noon–11pm (2.30am Fri-Sat)
Like the Excise Bar, The
Vaults caters mainly for
young people from the
world of business who
come here to relax and
play. Its fine stone vaulting
reflects its former role in
the field of international
trade, though at
weekends its nightclub
attracts pleasure-seekers
from all walks of life.

O'Reilly/Sub Lounge (D B4)
→ Tara St. Tel. 671 6769
Sun-Wed 4–11.30pm;
Thu-Sat 4pm–2.30am
Eventful evenings under
Tara Station in a mock-
Gothic pub, with the
vibration of the Dart trains
overhead and pop music
spun by DJs (Thu-Sat).

SHOPPING

Easons (D A4)
→ 40 O'Connell St
Tel. 858 3800 Daily 8.30am–
6.45pm (8.45pm Thu-Fri;
7.45pm Sat); Sun noon–6pm
No booklover should miss
the opportunity to visit to
one of the best bookstores

in Ireland, founded in the
19th century. Hundreds of
volume on several floors.

Talbot Street (D C3)
A long street of
second-hand stores with
gaudy signs advertising
their low prices – you can
buy a complete new outfit
for under €30.

Guiney & Co (no. 79)
→ Tel. 878 8835
A Dublin institution, with
shoes and coats – it's not
always very stylish, but
it's certainly cheap and
cheerful. Very friendly staff.

The Bag Shop (no. 10)
→ Tel. 873 1065
Bags in all shapes and
sizes, as well as rucksacks,
purses etc., at low prices.

Clery's (D A4)
→ 18-27 O'Connell St Lower
Tel. 878 6000 Daily 9am–
6.30pm (9pm Thu; 8pm Fri);
Sun noon–6pm
Umbrellas, souvenirs of all
kinds, hardware, lingerie
etc., Clery's department
store is sure to have
something for everyone.

Arnotts (D A4)
→ 12 Henry St. Tel. 872 1111
Mon-Sat 9am–6.30pm
(9pm Thu; 6pm Sat);
Sun noon–6pm
A large department store,
very popular with the
locals, recently refurbished
and with an enormous
range of goods for sale.

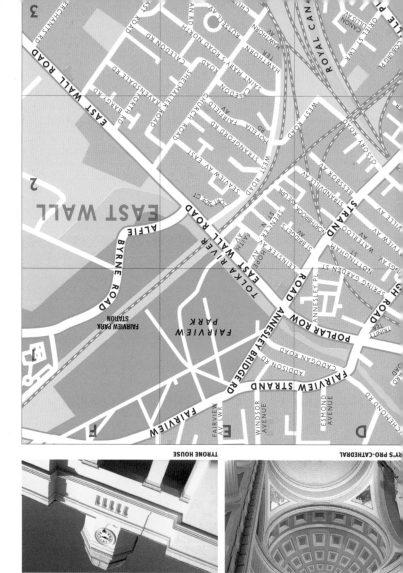

3

MERCHANTS RD

EAST WALL ROAD

EAST WALL

EAST WALL ROAD

2

ROYAL CAN

WEST ROAD

OSSORY ROAD

FAIRVIEW

FAIRVIEW PARK
STATION

FAIRVIEW
PARK

BYRNE ROAD

ALFIE

ALFIE BYRNE ROAD

TOLKA RIVER

EAST WALL ROAD

PARK SIDE CT

SEAVIEW AV EAST

WEST ROAD

STRANDVILLE AV

BESSBORO AV

NOTTINGHAM

WATERLOO AV

STRAND

SPRING GARDEN ST

POPLAR ROW

ANNESLEY PL

ANNESLEY BRIDGE RD

ROAD

CADOGAN ROAD

ADDISON RD

FAIRVIEW STRAND

WINDSOR
AVENUE

ESMOND
AVENUE

FAIRVIEW
AV WR

F

E

D

AN RD

CALEDON RD

SHELMALIER RD

RAVENSDALE RD

SAINT MARY'S ROAD NORTH

HAWTHORN

RUSSELL AV

CHI

KEDON ROAD

CHURCHILL TER

RICHMOND RD

MOFELIA

FAIRFIELD AV

STRANDFORD RD

WEST STREET

SEAVIEW AV EAST

SPENCER AV

ST BRIDGET'S AV

HOPE AV

LEINSTER AV

FAITH AV

BARRYS RD

CHELSA

CANON

SEVILLE PL

OSBORNE

 ST LWR

LEITRIM AV

VIEW AV

KINGS AV

NGS AV

GH ROAD

TRINITY TER

WINDSOR

AD

MERI

CHERMOND RD

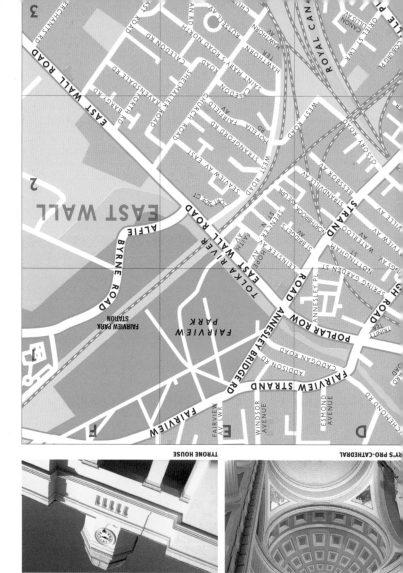

TYRONE HOUSE

RY'S PRO-CATHEDRAL

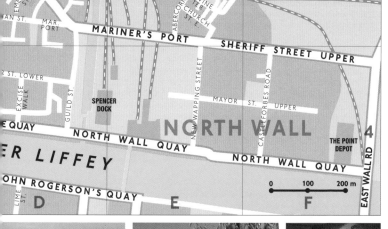

MARINER'S PORT
SHERIFF STREET UPPER
SPENCER DOCK
NORTH WALL
NORTH WALL QUAY
THE POINT DEPOT
ER LIFFEY
OHN ROGERSON'S QUAY
NORTH WALL QUAY
D E F

0 100 200 m

ATIONAL FINANCIAL SERVICES CENTRE

MOUNTJOY SQUARE

GAA MUSEUM

rth bank of the Liffey. e fire damage in 1921 mer customs' house, 1791, remains 's most beautiful istrative building. In eption area is an tion on the building's ct, James Gandon, e history of taxes.

Famine es (D C4)

'om House Quay awny bronze figures, ng and in tatters. ly realistic, they ize the terrible of 1846–50 which d Ireland. A fungus the potato crop, ng peasants of their stenance. More than one million Irish citizens died of stravation, typhus, scurvy or dysentery.

★ **International Financial Services Centre (D** C-D4) → *Bank of the Liffey, east of Amiens St* The city's business center is housed along the quays, Dublin's former docklands. Government redevelopment started in 1986, in order to complete a sector of the city that would be devoted to financial services. The plan was incredibly successful, and the IFSC district now operates at full throttle. This is a little city within a city, complete with its own offices, hotels, flats, bars and restaurants, and growing in size with every day that passes. Stretched out in a narrow belt along the riverbank, the IFSC is now expanding on the opposite side of the Liffey too in a landscape filled with mechanical diggers and towering cranes.

★ **Mountjoy Square (D** B2) The entrepreneur Gardiner, who became Viscount Mountjoy, gave his name to Dublin's greatest neoclassical square, one of the most fashionable of its time, before it was gradually deserted by the aristocracy. Around the garden, the gently curved balconies and the stunning front steps enhance the beauty of these buildings.

★ **GAA Museum Gaelic Athletic Association (D** B1) → *Croke Park. Tel. 819 2323 Mon-Sat 9.30am–5pm; Sun noon–5pm* The Irish passion for sport is documented in an interactive museum two steps from the stadiums. It shows videos of various champions of football, polo and hurling, and exhibits sports kits and medals since the war. Also, there's an excellent son-et-lumière show, followed by a series of absorbing games in which you can test your own reflexes.

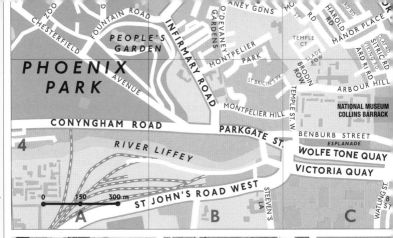

HUGH LANE GALLERY

HENRIETTA STREET

ST MARY'S ABBEY

★ **Glasnevin Cemetery (E** D1)

→ *Finglas Rd. Tel. 830 1133 Daily 9.30am–4.30pm*
Daniel O'Connell, Charles Stewart Parnell, Constance Markievicz, Brendan Behan and other celebrities rest in peace in Ireland's largest Catholic cemetery (1832). Over 120 acres, topsy-turvy crosses are juxtaposed with magnificent tombstones.

★ **James Joyce Centre (E** F3)

→ *35 North Great Georges St Tel. 878 8547 Mon–Fri 9.30am– 12.30pm, 1.30–3.30pm. www.jamesjoyce.ie*
Paying homage to one of the giants of Irish literature, this museum recalls Joyce's life

and work through photos, portraits, furniture and paintings of the 17 different homes in Dublin that his family once inhabited.

★ **Rotunda Hospital (E** F3)

→ *Parnell Square West Tel. 873 0700 (visits to the chapel by appointment)*
In 1745 Dr Mosse opened the world's first maternity hospital for mothers in need. Soon, the tiny old theater became too small and, in 1752, Dr Mosse bought four acres of land north of the river. His friend Richard Cassels applied his genius in designing the new building and its gardens. The pretty rotunda (80 ft in diameter), after

which the hospital takes its name, dates from 1764. Afternoon teas and functions held by the aristocracy financed the project. The park no longer exists, but the exquisite baroque chapel decorated with stucco-work cherubs does: it is one of the most exceptional places of worship in Dublin.

★ **Garden of Remembrance (E** F3)

→ *Parnell Square East*
These gardens commemorate Ireland's past. Don't miss the bronze statue to the memory of those who died fighting for freedom. The 1916 uprising blends curiously well with

Celtic myth: mosaics of spears in a cross-s pond, harp-shaped fe and statues of the Ch of Lir changing into sw (according to legend, metamorphosis would have lasted for 900 ye

★ **Dublin Writers Museum (E** F3)

→ *18 Parnell Square No Tel. 872 2077 Mon–Sat 5pm (6pm in summer e Sat); Sun 11am–5pm. www.writersmuseum.c*
Housed in the former Jameson Whiskey fam home this museum showcases Irish write their hours of glory. H and there, each one h his mark or a persona

★ **DUBLIN ZOO**

PRUSSIA STREET
AUGHRIM STREET
NORTH CIRCULAR ROAD
ST. OXMANTOWN
ROSS
MANOR MEWS
MARLBOROUGH

NORTH C
DRUMALEE RD
DRUMALEE RD

ANNAMOE
ELMSMERE AV
BLACKHORSE GROVE
GLENBEIGH GROVE
GLENBEIGH PARK
GLENBEIGH ROAD
CARLISLE CT
CARNAGH

OLD CABRA ROAD
CABRA DRIVE
ANNAMOE ROAD
MICKEE DR

BLACKHORSE AVENUE

DUNARD DR
DUNARD WALK
DUNARD DRIVE
DUNARD AVENUE
DUNARD ROAD

FISH POND
NORTH ROAD
NORTH ROAD

ANNAMOE
ANNAMOE TER
CABRA ROAD

CABRA

SCREEN RD
HAMPTON
SLEMISH ROAD

IMAAL RD
LEIX ROAD
ERRIS RD
QUARRY ROAD
OFFALY ROAD
ANNALY ROAD
FASSAUGH ROA

SWILLY ROAD
QUARRY ROAD
CARNLOUGH ROAD
DRUMCLIFFE ROAD
INVER RD
DINGLE ROAD

NAVAN ROAD

FASSAUGH ROAD
ST JARLATH ROAD
ST FINTAN RD
EITHNE RD
BANNOW ROAD
MULROY RD
KILKIERIAN RD
KILKIERIAN RD

DRUMCLIFFE RD
KILLALA ROAD
DUNMANUS ROAD
LISCANNOR ROAD
KILLARD RD

RATOATH ROAD
RATOATH RD
NEPHIN ROAD
NEPHIN ROAD

POPE JOHN PAUL II PARK
VENTRY ROAD

ST ATTRACTA ROAD
RO

Glasnevin / Parnell / Phoenix Park

ROTUNDA HOSPITAL

JAMES JOYCE CENTRE

GLASNEVIN CEMETERY

From Parnell Square to Glasnevin Cemetery, follow the trail of Dublin's famous characters: Belvedere College attended by James Joyce, the Writers Museum, and a memorial garden. To the west are rows of little streets along which stand, behind old façades, some of the most beautiful 18th-century townhouses, a legacy of the best architects of the time. Toward the south, the atmosphere suddenly brightens: bars, cafés and bookstores spring to life on Capel Street, then stretch out along the docks. To the extreme west is Phoenix Park, Europe's second biggest city park, with its cricket pitches, famous zoo and roaming deer.

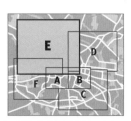

CHAPTER ONE

HALO

RESTAURANTS

Epicurian Food Hall (E F4**)**
→ 46 Abbey St Middle
Mon-Sat 9am–7.30pm
(8.30pm Thu-Fri; 6.30pm
Sat); Sun noon–6pm
Food hall dedicated to fine foods from all over the world. Numerous prepared dishes and tables are laid out for you to enjoy a brief visit to Turkey, Greece, Mexico, Spain or Japan, at a wide range of prices. Meals from €6.

Soup Dragon (E E4**)**
→ 168 Capel St
Tel. 872 3277 Mon-Fri 8am–
5.30pm; Sat 11am–5pm
Tiny bar serving every type of soup imaginable – chicken, fish, vegetable, cheese – freshly prepared each morning. The menu changes daily. Choice of three desserts.
À la carte €9.50.

The Oval Pub (E F4**)**
→ 78 Abbey St Middle
Tel. 872 1264 Mon-Sat
10.30am–11.30pm (12.30am
Thu-Sat); Sun 11am–11pm
Pub renowned for serving, on the first floor, the best Irish stew in the city. Delicious with brown bread. À la carte €10.

Chapter One (E F3**)**
→ 18-19 Parnell Square

Tel. 873 2266 Tue-Fri 12.30–
2.30pm, 6–11pm; Sat 6–
10.30pm; pre-theater menu
Tue-Sat 6–7pm
The best gastronomic restaurant on the north bank, located in the basement of the Writers Museum. The dining room is elegant and comfortable and, to match the decor, dishes are on the classic side, delicately enhanced with vegetables and good sauces, and accompanied with fine wines. À la carte €50; pre-theater three-course menu €31.

Halo (E F4**)**
→ Morrison Hotel, Ormond
Quay Lower. Tel. 887 2421
Daily noon–3pm, 6–10.30pm
The restaurant is part of the luxurious Morrison Hotel, an elegant and relaxing atmosphere featuring fine wood, mother-of-pearl, and gorgeous antique furniture. Its picture windows overlook Ormond Quay, a fascinating view to contemplate while dining on the finest fresh produce the city has to offer.
À la carte €40–50.

CAFÉ

Chapterhouse Café (E F3**)**
→ 18 Parnell Square
Tel. 872 2077 Mon-Sat
10am–5pm (6pm in summer)

SPIRIT

MOORE STREET MARKET

A place to unwind after a visit to the Writers' Museum or to enjoy the sun in good weather. Terrace with teak chairs.

PUBS, THEATER, CLUBS

Jack Nealon (E E4)
→ 165 Capel St
Tel. 872 3247
Mon-Thu 10.30am–11.30pm; Fri-Sat noon–12.30am; Sun 12.30–11pm
In the unlikely setting of a former synagogue transformed into a classic Irish pub, is this friendly, well-run bar of great comfort. Strange contrast between the packed bar and the calm area by the fireplace.

Slattery's (E E4)
→ 129 Capel St
Tel. 874 6844 Mon-Sat 11.30am–11.30pm (2.30am Fri-Sat); Sun 12.30–11pm
Attractive fashionable pub in a smart green building. Inside, the warmth of the decor invites you to wander around. Some of the city's best bands play music upstairs (Sat).

Sin é (E E4)
→ 14-15 Ormond Quay Upper
Tel. 878 7078 Mon-Sat noon–12.30am (2.30am Thu-Sat); Sun 1pm–midnight
A bar with a Gaelic name

('That's it!'), that is now one of the city's liveliest nightspots. Live DJs every night, friendly barmen to fetch your next pint, and state-of-the-art music with no concessions to the pop charts are the secrets of success here. Beware, it's busier than ever at weekends.

Pravda (E F4)
→ 35 Liffey St Lower
Tel. 874 0090 Mon-Sat noon–11.30pm (2.30am Thu-Sat); Sun 1–11pm
From its name it's easy to deduce that this is a bar with a Russian touch, including a fresco to the glory of the Red Army, photos of cold, snow-laden landscapes and various other Russian artefacts. Sit in one of the many small bar areas spread over the two floors and swap your beer for a vodka. Great atmosphere.

The Gate (E F3)
→ 1 Cavendish Row, Parnell Square. Tel. 874 4045
www.gate-theatre.ie
Works by Oscar Wilde, Orson Welles, James Mason as well as productions from the modern and classic Irish repertoire have been staged at this celebrated theater, a former refectory of the Rotunda Hospital.

Traffic (E F4)
→ 54 Middle Abbey St
Tel. 873 4038
Mon-Wed 3–11pm; Thu-Sun 3pm–2.30am (nightclub from 11pm)
A swanky club with chandeliers and white leather seats. The downstairs basement plays techno, house, electro and hardhouse, and, to catch your breath, there's a rather hip lounge bar on the first floor with a good cocktail list.

Spirit (E F4)
→ 57 Abbey St Middle
Tel. 877 9999
Thu-Sun 10.30am–4am
With two dance floors, three bars, a VIP balcony and even a massage parlor, Spirit is one of the hottest nightspots in town. There's music to suit everyone's taste, from hip-hop and dance in the basement to the cooler sounds of techno upstairs. The noise is absolutely deafening, and the crowds can't get enough of it.

GALLERY

The Bridge Art Gallery (E E4)
→ 6 Ormond Quay
Tel. 872 9702 Mon-Sat 10am–6pm; Sun 2–5pm
Exhibitions which change

on a monthly basis, showing the work of many types of artist (painters, ceramists etc.).

SHOPPING

Woolen Mills (E F4)
→ 41 Ormond Quay Lower
Tel. 828 0301 Mon-Sat 9.30am–5.30pm (5pm Sat)
Venerable shop (1888), where James Joyce worked for several years. Famous for its jumpers, scarves and pure-wool coats.

Chapters (E F4)
→ 108-109 Middle Abbey St
Tel. 872 3297
Mon-Sat 9.30am–6.20pm (10am Thu); Sun noon–6pm
Those who seek shall find – at very low prices. Piles of books, DVDs and CDs spread over four floors.

Moore Street Market (E F4)
→ Mon-Sat 9am–5pm
Dublin's most authentic market. Fruit, vegetables, fish, irons, radios and a variety of bizarre items.

Jervis Center (E E4)
→ Jervis St. Tel. 878 1323
Mon-Sat 9am–6pm (9pm Thu); Sun noon–6pm
A wide range of goods in around fifty stores and boutiques, housed in one of Dublin's busiest and most consumer-friendly shopping malls.

BELVEDERE COLLEGE JAMES JOYCE CENTRE
DUBLIN WRITERS MUSEUM
HUGH LANE GALLERY

GARDINER ST. UPR
TEMPLE ST.
ST. UPR DORSET
DORSET ST. LWR
DORSET ST. UPR
BELVEDERE PL. UPR
ECCLES PLACE
ECCLES STREET
LEO ST.
INNISFALLEN PAR.
WILLIAM'S PL. UPR
GLENGARIFF PAR.

NELSON ST.
ST. IGNATIUS ROAD

WELLINGTON ST.
PRIMROSE ST.
AUBURN ST.
BERKELEY ST.
GERALDINE ST.
GOLDSMITH ST.

ROYAL CANAL BANK
CITY BASIN

WESTERN WAY
PHIBSBOROUGH ROAD
PHIBSBOROUGH

ANGLESEA RD.
RATHDOWN RD.
NORGEGMAN UPPER
MONCK PLACE
SOUTH
GREAT WESTERN
AVONDALE AV.
GREAT WESTERN
CABRA ROAD

BERKELEY RD
NORTH CIRCULAR RD
MATER MISERICORDIA HOSPITAL

PROSPECT ROAD
ST PETER'S PK
DALYMOUNT PARK
CABRA PK
NORFOLK RD
ST PETER'S RD
CONNAUGHT
ULSTER STREET
MUNSTER STREET
LEINSTER ST. N.
SHANDON DR.
SHANDON PARK

DRUMCONDRA STATION
ROYAL CANAL
ROYAL CANAL BANK

ST PATRICK'S RD
ST COLUMBA'S RD
WHITWORTH RD
CLAUDE RD
WIGAN RD
WIGAN RD
DAVID
ALPHONSUS ROAD
CRAWFORD AVENUE
GARTAN AV.
IONA ROAD
LINDSAY ROAD
DALCASSIAN DOWNS

DRUMCONDRA
CARLINGFORD ROAD
DARGLE RD
HOLLYBANK ROAD
MANNIX RD
BOTANIC AV.
IONA CRES.
IONA PARK
IONA PARK
IONA DR.
MARGUERITE ROAD
IONA VILLAS

GRIFFITH PARK
BOTANIC ROAD
PROSPECT AV.
FINGLAS ROAD
BOTANIC ROAD
GLASNEVIN CEMETERY
CLAREVILLE GROVE
PROSPECT AV.

GARDEN OF REMEMBRANCE

DUBLIN WRITERS MUSEUM

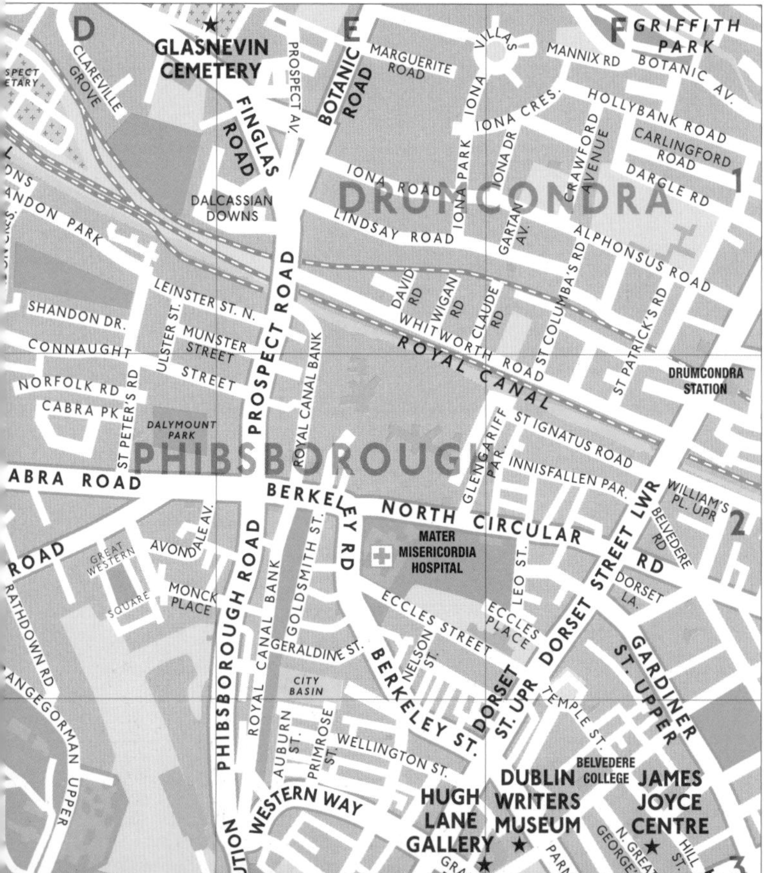

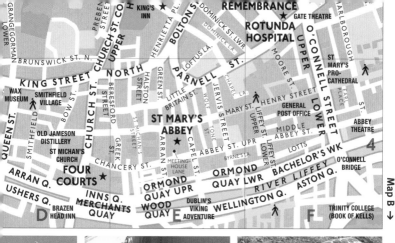

FOUR COURTS

DUBLIN ZOO

nir: Shaw's signature, hain's spectacles, a dition of Bram Stoker's *a*, Joyce's piano and tt's telephone. Also a portrait gallery and s filled with books.

gh Lane
ry (E E3)
rlemont House,
Square North
5550
t 9.30am–6pm (5pm
; Sun 11am–5pm
sidence of the Count rlemont (by the ct Chambers, 1762) s an international art y of 19th-century to nt-day paintings. The f the collection is up of works donated by enthusiast Hugh Lane (d. 1915). Watercolors by Jack Butler Yeats (brother of the poet), English and French Impressionists, abstract-art videos and temporary exhibitions by contemporary artists.

★ Henrietta Street (E E3)
A row of dilapidated buildings in Dublin's oldest Georgian street (1720). At the top end is the imposing King's Inn, designed by James Gandon in 1795 as a residence for young lawyers, though today the building is a training school for magistrates. The elegant lines took 22 years and several architects to complete.

★ St Mary's Abbey (E E4)
→ *Meetinghouse Lane*
Tel. 647 2461 Wed-Sat 10am–5pm (mid June-mid Sep)
The remains of the largest Cistercian monastery in Ireland, founded in 1139 and destroyed by Henry VIII in 1537. To visit the chapterhouse, descend 6½ ft underground to the actual level of the city in the Middle Ages.

★ Four Courts (E D4)
→ *Inns Quay*
Mon-Fri 10am–1pm, 2–4pm
A dome and four buildings designed in 1785 by Gandon to house the high courts. In 1922, republicans hostile to the Anglo-Irish Treaty, occupied the building. After a week of shelling by the

Treaty's supporters, the building was destroyed and its archives burnt. The current building that today looks out onto the Liffey is a copy (1932). It houses Ireland's High and Supreme courts.

★ Dublin Zoo (E A3)
→ *Phoenix Park. Tel. 474 8900*
Mon-Sat 9.30am–6pm (sunset in Nov-Feb); Sun 10.30am–6pm (sunset in Nov-Feb)
The lion used in MGM movie credits would doubtless have been raised in one of the oldest zoos in Europe, where, since 1830, exotic animals have lived in these cages. Follow the winding paths to the cages of pandas and arctic foxes.

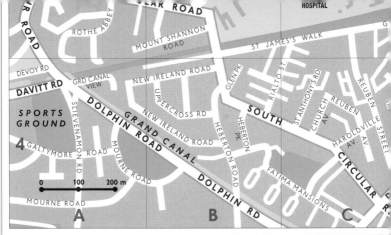

(Map area with labels: LEAR ROAD, HOSPITAL, ROTHE ABBEY, MOUNT SHANNON ROAD, ST JAMES'S WALK, DEVOY RD, GRD CANAL VIEW, NEW IRELAND ROAD, GLEN PK, RIALTO ST, ST ANTHONY'S RD, REUBEN, DAVITT RD, UPPERCROSS RD, SOUTH, CHURCH AV, HAROLDVILLE AV, REUBEN STREET, SPORTS GROUND, SLIEVENAMON RD, DOLPHIN ROAD, GRAND CANAL, NEW IRELAND ROAD, HEBERTON RD, HEBERTON PK, CIRCULAR, GALTYMORE ROAD, MOURNE ROAD, FATIMA MANSIONS, DOLPHIN RD, MOURNE ROAD)

0   100   200 m

A   B   C

NATIONAL MUSEUM COLLINS BARRACKS

HEUSTON STATION

ROYAL HOSPITAL

★ St Michan's Church (F F1)

→ Church St. Tel. 872 4154
Mon–Fri 10am–12.45pm,
2–4.45pm (12.30–3pm Nov–
Feb); Sat 10am–12.45pm
Legend has it that the Danes
founded this church in 1095
for their saints. Handel is
said to have rehearsed his
Messiah on the clavier here
in front of a vast audience.
The penitents pew once
served as a place to publicly
confess your wrongdoings.
Accessed through a narrow
trapdoor in the crypt, four
natural mummies have laid
for centuries: the walls
impregnated with methane
have preserved them
without embalming.

★ Old Jameson Distillery (F F1)

→ Bow St, Smithfield
Tel. 807 2355
Daily 9am–5.30pm.
www.jameson.ie
Closed in 1970, this
fascinating whiskey
distillery reveals the recipes
used since the 6th century.
Bubbling vats and wax
figures give the illusion that
the factory is still in
operation. Follow the
preparation of this nectar
from barley grain through
maturation, then finish with
sample tastings. At the top
of the chimney is Dublin's
highest observatory point
and beautiful panoramic
views of the city.

★ Smithfield Village (F E1)

→ CEOL. Tel. 817 3820
The old distillery district
is changing fast. However
if it now boasts modern
buildings, it has kept its
little houses, the chimney-
observatory of its former
distillery and even the noisy
horsefair held on the first
Sunday of every month.
On the cobbled square,
horsetraders and children
bid at the tops of their
voices in a setting straight
out of a western. In summer,
an unforgettable festival
based on Celtic song and
dance is held at the Centre
for Traditional Irish
Music (CEOL).

★ Guinness Storehouse (F D2)

→ St James's Gate
Tel. 408 4800 Daily 9.3...
5pm (8pm July-Aug).
www.guinnessstorehou...
Terrific interactive mu...
of Ireland's most fam...
brewery, located in a ...
hop warehouse (the t...
building in Dublin),
renovated in 2001 by ...
Architects. Spread ov...
floors and punctuated
the sound of machine...
exhibitions, movies a...
even cascades of pur...
from the Wicklow
mountains, the very
beginnings of the tas...
Guinness. Sample a f...
pint of the black stuff

ST MICHAN'S CHURCH

OLD JAMESON DISTILLERY

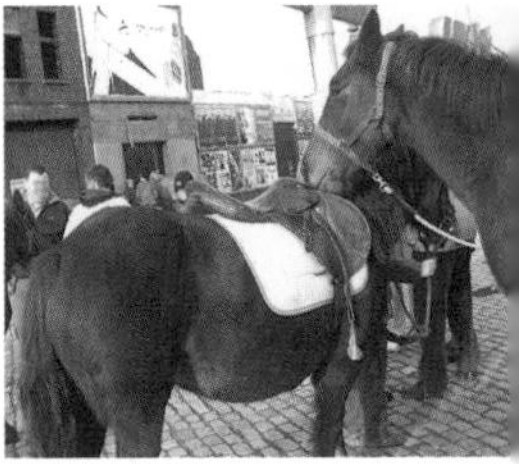

SMITHFIELD VILLAGE

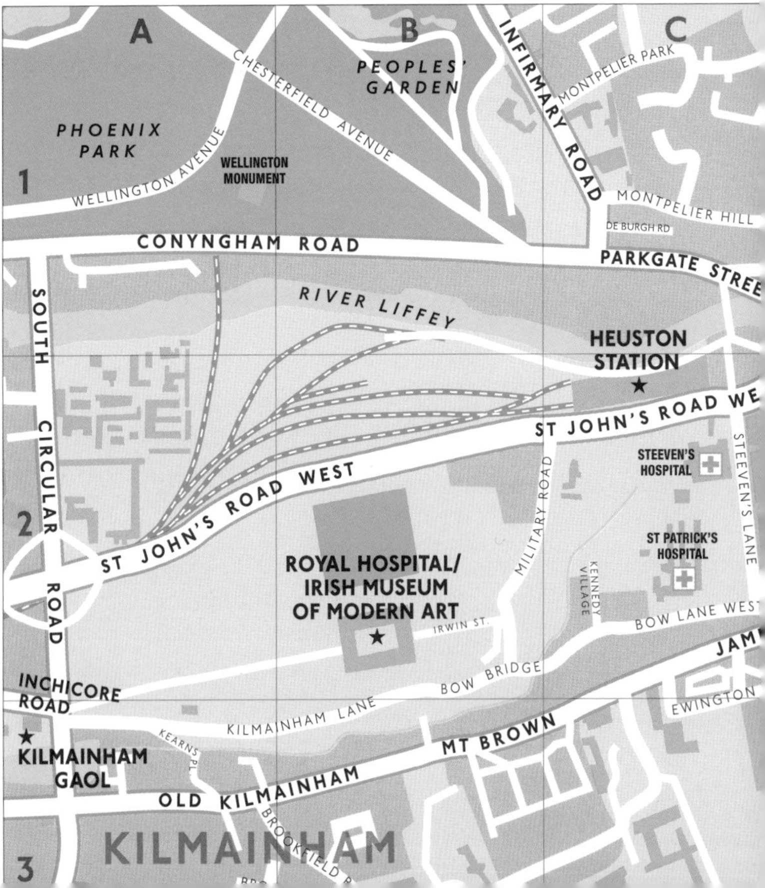

A   B   C

CHESTERFIELD AVENUE

PEOPLES'
GARDEN

INFIRMARY ROAD

MONTPELIER PARK

PHOENIX
PARK

WELLINGTON AVENUE

WELLINGTON
MONUMENT

1

WELLINGTON AVENUE

MONTPELIER HILL

DE BURGH RD

CONYNGHAM ROAD

PARKGATE STREE

RIVER LIFFEY

HEUSTON
STATION
★

SOUTH CIRCULAR ROAD

ST JOHN'S ROAD WE

ST JOHN'S ROAD WEST

STEEVEN'S
HOSPITAL ✚

STEEVEN'S LANE

MILITARY ROAD

2

ROYAL HOSPITAL/
IRISH MUSEUM
OF MODERN ART
★

ST PATRICK'S
HOSPITAL ✚

KENNEDY VILLAGE

BOW LANE WEST

IRWIN ST

INCHICORE
ROAD

BOW BRIDGE

JAM

KILMAINHAM LANE

KEARNS

MT BROWN

EWINGTON

KILMAINHAM
GAOL

OLD KILMAINHAM

BROOKFIELD

3

KILMAINHAM

The western side of the city has an industrial appearance, thanks to the manufacture of whiskey and beer. The Guinness Brewery and the Old Jameson Distillery stand on either side of the Liffey, with the fumes of the former filling the air with a delicious scent, and the latter overshadowing the newly refurbished Smithfield Village. This is a fascinating part of the city to explore, filled with studios, restaurants, cafés, gift shops and old-fashioned cottages.

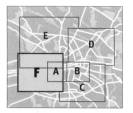

CHIEFS O'NEILLS

KELLY AND PING RESTAURANT

RESTAURANTS

Grass Roots Café (F B2)
→ *Irish Museum of Modern Art, Royal Hospital*
Tel. 474 1451 Mon-Sat 10am–5pm; Sun noon–5pm
A typical museum of modern art café, with chairs and metallic tables in geometric shapes and brightly-colored flowers on the tables. Tasty lunches can be enjoyed at reasonable prices: quiches, lasagne, salads, generous portions of pie or sponge cake. Main course and dessert €10.

The Still Room (F F1)
→ *Old Jameson Distillery, Smithfield*
Tel. 807 2355 Daily 9am–5pm (hot food until 2.30pm, sandwiches all day)
Hearty Irish and continental fare in generous portions are eaten inside the distillery itself, under the enormous distressed wooden beams and red brick. Friendly service and a unique location. À la carte €11.

Bu-Ali (F F4)
→ *28 Clanbrassil St Lower*
Tel. 454 6505
Daily 5–11.30pm
A delicious smell of spices hits your nostrils as soon as you enter this tiny, informal restaurant offering excellent Indian food: marinated beef, vegetarian curry, lemon rice, stuffed nans etc. Eat in or take out. À la carte €13.

Chiefs O'Neills (F E1)
→ *Smithfield Village*
Tel. 817 3838 Mon-Fri noon–10pm; Sat 5–10pm
The hotel-restaurant of Chief O'Neills is renowned throughout Smithfield. The dining room is large, airy and restful, with blue-tinted lighting. On offer are slow-cooked meats, fish dishes and a very tempting dessert trolley. €15.

Nancy Hand (F C1)
→ *30-32 Parkgate St*
Tel. 677 0149
Daily 10.30am–11.30pm (1.30am Fri-Sat)
On the bank of the Liffey, and worth the walk from the city center, is this traditional pub on a par with the best restaurants in Parkgate St. Salmon with red chili, fish mousse, duck with peaches are some of the dishes served on the wooden mezzanine, above the bar. There are 60 types of whiskey and vodka on offer. À la carte €20–30.

Kelly and Ping Restaurant (F E1)
→ *Smithfield Village*
Tel. 817 3840 Mon-Fri noon–10pm; Sat 5–10.30pm
A mixture of Irish and

THE DUBLIN BREWING COMPANY

KEARNS

Oriental cuisine, with a decor to match. Potato cakes, chicken with peanuts, tofu curry, and beer ice cream (yes!). Attentive service. À la carte €25–30.

CAFÉ, BARS, PUBS

Brambles Café (F D1)
→ *National Museum Collins Barracks. Tel. 633 4280 Tue-Sat 9.30am–5pm; Sun 1–5pm*
Opening onto the square courtyard of the garrison is this small and welcoming café which has been tastefully designed to complement the style of the Collins Barracks: whitewashed walls and and earthenware pots.

Gravity Bar (F D2)
→ *Guinness Storehouse, St James's Gate Tel. 408 4800 Daily 9.30am–5pm (8pm July-Aug)*
The bar in the Guinness Storehouse is perched high in the sky like a flight control tower, or a giant saucer sitting right on top of the building. It offers a unique all-round view of the city and beyond. Your entry ticket to the museum, incidentally, includes the price of a pint of the best Guinness you'll ever taste.

The Tap Bar (F F1)
→ *44 King St North Tel. 872 1772 Mon-Sat 11am–11.30pm (12.30am Fri; 2am Sat); Sun 11.30am–11pm*
This lounge bar with comfortable leather armchairs is a great favorite with the residents of Smithfield. Traditional live music (Thu nights).

1780 Bar (F E1)
→ *New Church St, Smithfield Tel. 817 2475 Daily noon–11.30pm*
The perfect place for whiskey enthusiasts (it's in the basement of the Old Jameson Distillery), with 25 to 30 different brands, from the youngest to the most mature – the famous Middleton. Light food is served all day.

Ryan's (F C1)
→ *28 Parkgate St Tel. 677 6097 Mon-Thu noon–11.30pm; Fri-Sat noon–1.30am; Sun noon–11pm*
On the way to Phœnix Park, one of Dublin's oldest pubs and, with its circular bar, one of the rarest of its kind. Friendly atmosphere and always packed.

Cobblestone Pub (F E1)
→ *77 North King St Tel. 872 1799 Mon-Sat 4–11.30pm (12.30am Fri-Sat);*

Sun 1–11pm
A sea-green sign on a pub whose worn exterior isn't much to look at, but inside the sound of violins, guitars, flutes and Irish bagpipes sing out every night. As far as traditional Irish music is concerned, this is the real thing.

Dice Bar (F E1)
→ *Queen St, Smithfield Village. Tel. 872 8622 Daily 5–11.30pm (2.30am Thu-Sat)*
Tucked away in one corner of this little narrow bar, the DJ here plays an eclectic mix of the latest sounds. Hip-hop, electro-rock and retro disco blend happily together in this easy-going and dimly-lit venue recalling any one of the trendy nightclubs around Manhattan's East Village.

Voodoo Lounge (F E2)
→ *39 Arran Quay Tel. 873 6013 Daily 5–11.30pm (2.30am Thu-Sat)*
A sweltering atmosphere, oceans of Guinness, live concerts and events every night are all on tap in this popular quayside venue halfway between Medieval City and Smithfield Village. Music every evening – disco, pop, house, New York lounge, hip-hop and reggae.

SHOPPING

Mary's Lane (F F1)
→ *Mon-Fri 4am–3pm; Sat 7.30am–11am*
A huge brick marketplace housing a fruit, vegetable and flower market selling produce from Ireland and elsewhere in the world.

The Dublin Brewing Company (F E1)
→ *141-146 King St North Tel. 872 5127 Mon-Fri noon–6pm (guided tours every hour, on the hour). www.dublinbrewing.com*
Brewery opened in 1996 whose stouts, ales and lagers have names such as *Maeve's, Beckett's* and *Revolution 1798*. Free tasting at the bar after the visit.

Kearns (F E1)
→ *69 Queen St. Tel. 677 3338 Tue-Sat 9am–5.30pm*
This jewelry store is also a pawnbroker's. New and second-hand pieces can be tried on in individual booths.

Royal Kilmainham Bookshop (F B2)
→ *Irish Museum of Modern Art. Tel. 612 9900 Mon-Sat 10am–5.30pm; Sun noon–5.30pm*
Stunning illustrated books on 20th-century artists, amusing diaries and clever games for children.

USEUM

GUINNESS STOREHOUSE

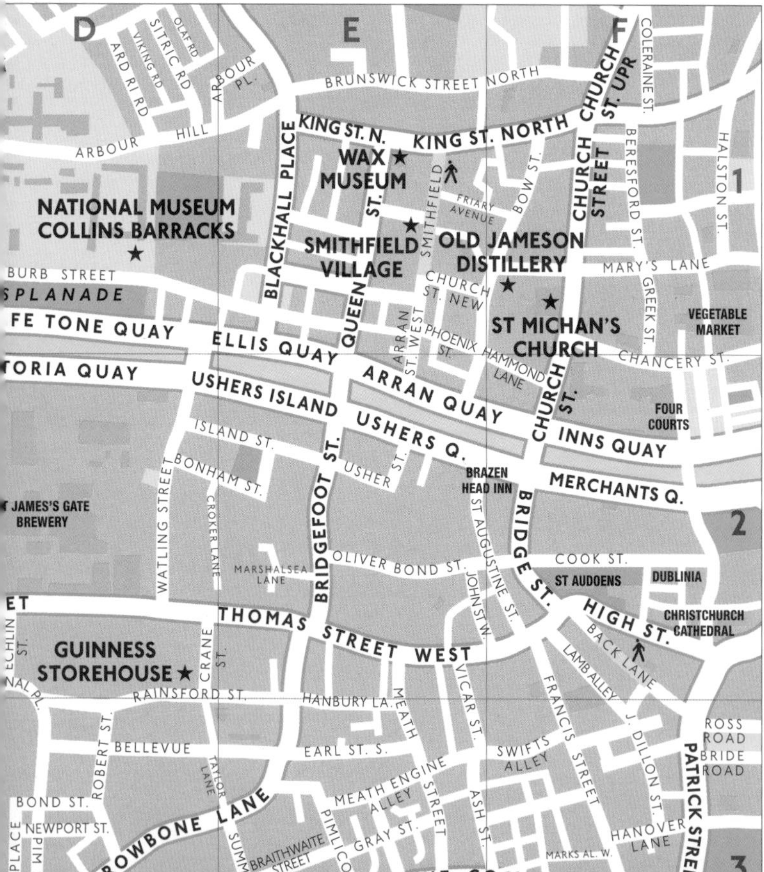

D E F

COLERAINE ST.
SITRIC RD
VIKING RD
ARD RI RD
ORFORD

ARBOUR PL.

BRUNSWICK STREET NORTH

ARBOUR HILL

KING ST. N. KING ST. NORTH

BLACKHALL PLACE

CHURCH STREET

CHURCH ST. UPR

BERESFORD ST.
HALSTON ST.

WAX MUSEUM ★

NATIONAL MUSEUM COLLINS BARRACKS ★

SMITHFIELD

BOW ST.

FRIARY AVENUE

1

BURB STREET

SMITHFIELD VILLAGE ★

QUEEN ST.

CHURCH ST. NEW

★ **OLD JAMESON DISTILLERY**

MARY'S LANE

GREEK ST.

SPLANADE

CHURCH ST. WEST

FE TONE QUAY

ELLIS QUAY

ARRAN ST. WEST

PHOENIX ST.

HAMMOND LANE

★ **ST MICHAN'S CHURCH**

CHANCERY ST.

VEGETABLE MARKET

TORIA QUAY

USHERS ISLAND

ARRAN QUAY

USHERS Q.

CHURCH ST.

INNS QUAY

FOUR COURTS

ISLAND ST.

BONHAM ST.

USHER ST.

BRIDGEFOOT ST.

USHER ST.

BRAZEN HEAD INN

BRIDGE ST.

MERCHANTS Q.

2

★ JAMES'S GATE BREWERY

WATLING STREET

CROKER LANE

MARSHALSEA LANE

OLIVER BOND ST.

JOHN ST. W.

ST AUGUSTINE ST.

COOK ST.

ST AUDOENS

HIGH ST.

DUBLINIA

CHRISTCHURCH CATHEDRAL

ET

GUINNESS STOREHOUSE ★

THOMAS STREET WEST

CRANE ST.

BACK LANE

LAMB ALLEY

NAL PL.

RAINSFORD ST.

HANBURY LA.

MEATH ST.

VICAR ST.

FRANCIS STREET

J. DILLON ST.

ROSS ROAD

BRIDE ROAD

ELHIN ST.

BELLEVUE

ROBERT ST.

TAYLOR LANE

EARL ST. S.

MEATH ENGINE ALLEY

ASH ST.

SWIFTS ALLEY

PATRICK STREE

BOND ST.

NEWPORT ST.

PLACE S MS

ROWBONE LANE

SUMME

BRAITHWAITE STREET

PIMLICO

GRAY ST.

MARKS AL. W.

HANOVER LANE

THE COO

3

→ Map C

HOSPITAL / IRISH MUSEUM OF MODERN ART

KILMAINHAM GAOL

Bar, perched high the city, with glass ws from floor to . Great views if you suffer from vertigo.

tional Museum s Barracks (F D1)
→ *burb St*
7444 Tue-Sat
5pm; Sun 2–5pm
d in the austere ks of General Collins museum (an annex National Museum) ted to the decorative ncient and modern. e pendulum, several high, creaks nically in the stairwell. ive trinkets of all 18th-century shoes, o year-old Japanese clock, modern furniture etc.

★ **Wax Museum (F** E1)
→ *Smithfield Square*
Mon-Sat 10am–5.30pm;
Sun noon–5.30pm
The waxworks here are often kitsch: showbiz personalities, political figures, tyrants and apostles all curiously arranged in poses recreating daily life. The brave can visit the chamber of horrors. For children there's a hall of mirrrors, rope bridges, dry ice and sound effects.

★ **Heuston Station (F** C2)
→ *St John's Rd West*
This 19th-century station, a model of elegance, is now a classified historic monument. Built in 1844,

its design was famed throughout Europe

★ **Royal Hospital/ Irish Museum of Modern Art (F** B2)
→ *Military Rd, Kilmainham*
Tel. 612 9900 Tue-Sat 10am–
5.30pm; Sun noon–5.30pm
The military hospital is a 1684 masterpiece inspired by Les Invalides in Paris, with four well laid-out wings, a clocktower and a cloister leading to the French gardens. The mess hall and baroque chapel ceiling, sculptured with fruit and vegetables, is open to the public in summer. Since 1991 the hospital has housed the collections of the National Museum of

Modern Art, consisting of almost 4,000 paintings, photographs, videos, sculptures and installations from the 1940s to the present day, displayed in permanent and temporary exhibitions.

★ **Kilmainham Gaol (F** A3)
→ *Inchicore Rd*
Tel. 453 5984 Daily 9.30am–
4.45pm. Oct-March: Mon-Fri
9.30am–4pm; Sun 10am–5pm
Six-person cells and extreme humidity, the disciplinary section gives an idea of the fate of prisoners here (1796–1924). Parnell, Emmet, Pearse and other political leaders were detained here or executed in the courtyard.

DART STATION

PLAN DU LUAS

LUAS

→ Tel. 1 800 300 604
From € 1.40.
Combined ticket bus-Luas,
valid 24 hrs: €6.20
Dublin's tramway (*luas*
means 'fast' in Gaelic).
Two lines – one red, one
green – that do not
intersect.

TAXIS

Indicated by a sign on
the roof which is lit when
the taxi is free. Hail them
in the street or book by
telephone 24 hours
a day.
City Cabs Tel. 872 7272
Taxi Seven Tel. 460 0000
Co-op Taxis Tel. 676 6666

CARS

Drive on the left of the
road.
Parking
Do not park on a double
yellow line. Parking lots
are indicated by blue
signs giving the number
of free spaces. Maps are
available from hotels.
Speed limits
→ 55 mph on main roads
→ 30 mph in city center
Car rental
There are several
agencies at the airport,
which all have branches
in the center of town.

BIKES

A wonderful way to
discover Dublin's
suburbs.
Rental
Deposit €200.
→ *Cycleways* (**E** E4)
185-186 Parnell St
Tel. 873 4748
20 €/day, 80 €/week.

in a dormitory.
Abbey Court (**D** A4)
→ 29 Bachelors Walk
Tel. 878 0700
www.abbey-court.com
A smart blue and orange
façade, small courtyard for
use on sunny days, a lively
cafeteria and a huge icebox
in the communal kitchen.
Dormitories of 4 to 12 beds,
€18–26 per person, €76
for two.
Brewery Hostel (**F** E2)
→ 22-23 Thomas St
Tel. 453 8600
www.irish-hostel.com
Warm, inviting decor, if a
little old fashioned, in the
style of the Guinness
brewery. Terraced lounge
with piano and open
fireplace. From €18.

€30–60

**Marian Guest
House** (**D** A2)
→ 21 Gardiner St Upper
Tel. 874 4129
www.marianguesthouse.ie
Friendly, informal Bed &
Breakfast in a three-story
bourgeois residence.
Shower and washroom on
each landing, sugar pink
wallpaper, pleasant
bedrooms with cupboards,
and a quiet courtyard.
€40–60.
**Phoenix Park
House** (**F** C1)
→ 38-39 Parkgate St
Tel. 677 2870
www.dublinguesthouse.com
Bed & Breakfast opposite
Phoenix Park. Thirty rooms
with patchwork quilts and
chests of drawers. For
breakfast, egg, bacon and
cereals served in a peach-
colored dining room. €66.
The Kingsbridge (**F** C1)
→ 14 Parkgate St
Tel. 677 3263
A tiny Bed & Breakfast with
old-fashioned charm. In
winter, a wood fire crackles
in the breakfast room.
Family atmosphere. € 75.

Charleville Lodge (**D** B2)
→ 268 North Circular Rd
Tel. 838 6633
www.charlevillelodge.ie
A luxury hotel at modest
prices in an elegant
Victorian residence a little
way out from the city
center. Elegant decor and
every comfort. €80.
Clifden House (**D** A2)
→ 32 Gardiner's Place
Tel. 874 6364
www.clifdenhouse.com
A boarding house in a
building in the Georgian old
city center. All rooms have
ensuite bathrooms and
those on the top floor have
baths. From €80.
The Harcourt Hotel (**C** B3)
→ 60 Harcourt St
Tel. 478 3677
www.harcourthotel.ie
This is the house where
George Bernard Shaw
wrote his play *Pygmalion*.
It is now divided into
98 modern rooms with
couches in the best ones.

DUBLIN AIRPORT

→ *7 miles north of the city*
Tel. 814 1111
www.dublin-airport.com
City center links
By bus
→ *Dublin bus*
*Lines no. 16A, 41B, 46X,
58X, 230, 746, 74 and 748;
journey time: 45 mins to
1 hr; price: €1.55 one way.*
→ *Airlink*
*To Busaras bus station in
20–35 mins; price: €6 one
way.*
→ *Aircoach*
*Daily, 24hrs; very
comfortable; journey time:
30–40 mins to Grafton St;
price: €7 one way.*
By taxi
Approx. 20 mins; €20–35.

MAIN ROUTES IN AND OUT OF DUBLIN

*Accommodation in Dublin
tends to be expensive but
much in demand so bookings
should be made as early as
possible, particularly June to
mid-September and
Christmas. Also, it is easier to
stay in the north of the city.
Except where otherwise
indicated the prices given are
for a double room with
bathroom in low season (tax
and breakfast included). There
is a difference between
hotels, guesthouses and Bed
& Breakfasts, many of which
close from December 20 to
the beginning of January.*

UNIVERSITY ACCOMMODATION

Trinity College (B D1)
→ *Tel. 7608 1177 June-Sep*
www.tcd.ie/accommodation
Apartments and rooms
at Trinity College, with
bathrooms on the same
floor. From €60 per person
for a room, €120 for two.

FLATS

**Oliver St John Gogarty
apartments (B** B1)
→ *18-21 Anglesea St*
Tel. 671 1822
www.gogartys.ie
Six apartments with from
one to three bedrooms
each, located in
penthouses at Temple Bar,
in the city center. Its central
situation and terrific views
means you should reserve
a long time in advance.
On the ground floor is the
famous pub of the same
name, and next door is
some excellent budget
accommodation in a series
of dormitories. €105–190
(apartments for two to six
guests), €15–30 (hostel).

YOUTH HOSTELS

*Private youth hostels are
members of the IHH
(Independent Holiday Hostels
organization). They offer*
dormitories and single and
double rooms at very good
prices compared to the
equivalent accommodation
elsewhere. No age limit.
**Isaacs Hostel
& Jacobs Inn (D** B3)
→ *2-5 Frenchman's Lane*
Tel. 855 6215
→ *21-28 Talbot Place*
Tel. 855 5660
www.isaacs.ie
Excellent value for money
at these two simple
hostels: wide spaces,
washing machine, well-
equipped kitchen and a
good location in a quiet
street. Cosmopolitan and
friendly atmosphere.
From €13–16 (dormitory),
and €56 for two in a
double room.
Avalon House (A F4)
→ *55 Aungier St*
Tel. 475 0001
www.avalon-house.ie
Stunning 19th-century
building, always busy.
Well-equipped cozy rooms

and various games on offer
(pool table, pinball
machine). Dormitory
€15–25; rooms from €35
per person.
Kinlay House (A E2)
→ *2-12 Lord Edward St*
Tel. 679 6644
www.kinlayhouse.ie
First-class hostel
accommodation
overlooking Christ Church
Cathedral in light and airy
dormitories containing
4 to 24 beds. Kinlay House
caters for the international
backpacking set, who all
seem very happy to be
here. €16–28 per person,
€56 for two.
**Dublin International
Youth Hostel (E** E3)
→ *61 Mountjoy St
(between Wellington St Upper
and Wellington St Lower)*
Tel. 830 4555
www.anoige.ie
The only state-owned youth
hostel, situated in a former
convent. €18 per person

Transportation and hotels in Dublin

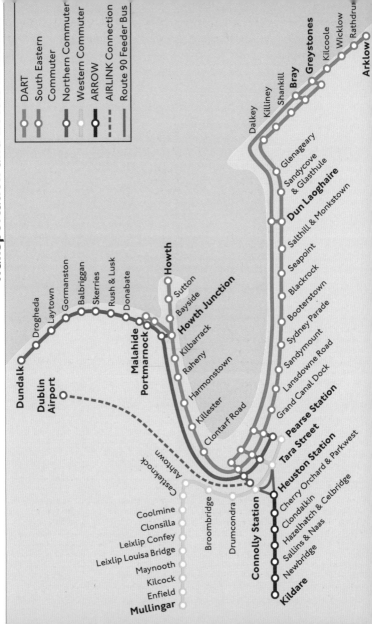

Street names, monuments and places to visit are listed alphabetically. They are followed by a map reference of which the initial letter in bold (**A, B, C...**) relates to the district and matching map.

Streets

Abbey St Lower D A4-B4
Abbey St Middle D A4
Abbey St Old D B4
Abbey St Upper E E4-F4
Abercorn Road D E3
Adelaide Road C B3-C4
Albert Court E. C E2
Albert Place E. C E2
Albert Place W. C B4
Amiens St D C3-C4
Andrew St B B2
Anglesea St B B1-B2
Anne St B C3
Anne's Lane B C3
Annesley Bridge Road D E1
Arbour Hill E C4, F D1
Arbour Place E C4, F D1-E1
Ard Ri Road E C3-C4, F D1
Ardee Row A B4
Ardee St A B4, F E3
Arran Quay A B1, E D4, F E2
Arran St E E4
Arran St E. A E1, E E4
Arran St W. F E1-E2
Ash St A C4, F E3
Aston Place B B1
Aston Quay B B1, D A4, E F4
Athlumney Villas C B4
Auburn St E E3
Aughrim St E B3-C3
Aungier Place B A4
Aungier St A F3-F4,
B A3-A4, C B2
Avondale Av. E D2
Bachelors Walk D A4, E F4
Back Lane A C2-D3, F F2
Baggot Court C D3
Baggot Lane C F3
Baggot St Lower C D3-E3
Baggot St Upper C E3
Ballybough Road D C2-D1
Bannow Road E C1
Bargy Road D F2-F3
Barrow St C F2
Basin St Upper F C3-D3
Bass Place C E2
Bath Lane D A2

Bayview Av. D D2
Beaver St D C3
Bedford Lane B B1
Bella St D C2
Bellevue Earl St S. F D3-E3
Belvedere Court D A2-B2
Belvedere Road D A1, E F2
Benburb St E C4, F D1
Beresford Place D B4
Beresford St E D4-E4, F F1
Berkeley Road E E2
Berkeley St E E2-E3
Bessbor Av. D D2
Bishop St C A2
Black Pitts F F4
Blackberry Lane C B4
Blackhall Parade E D4
Blackhall Place E C4-D4, F E1
Blackhorse Av. E A2-B3
Blackhorse Grove E B2
Bloomfield Av. C A4
Bolton St E E3
Bond St F D3
Bonham St A A1, F D2-E2
Botanic Av. E F1
Botanic Road E E1
Bow Bridge F B2
Bow Lane E. B A4
Bow Lane W. F C2
Bow St A B1, E D4, F E1-F1
Boyne St C D1-E1
Brabazon Row A B4, F E3
Braithwaite St A A4, F E3
Brickfield Lane F E3-E4
Bride Road A D3-E3, C A2, F F3
Bride St A E3-E4, C A2-A3
Bridge St A C1-C2, F F2
Bridgefoot St A A1-A2, F E2
Brodin Row E C4, F C1-D1
Brookfield Road F A3-B3
Brookfield St F A3-B3
Brown St S. F D4-E4
Brunswick St N. E D4, F E1-F1
Buckingham St D C2-C3
Bull Alley St A D3-E3, C A2
Burlington Road C D4-E4
Cabra Drive E B2-C2
Cabra Park E D2

Cabra Road E B2-D2
Cadogan Road D D1-E1
Caledon Road D E3-F3
Camden Place C B3
Camden Row C A3-B3
Camden St Lower C B3
Camden St Upper C B3
Canal Road C B4
Capel St A E1-F1, E E4
Caragh Road E B2
Cardiff Lane C E1-F1
Carlingford Road E F1
Carlisle St C A3
Carnlough Road E B1-B2
Castle St A E2-F2, C A1
Castleforbes Road D F4
Cathedral St D A3
Cathedral View Wk C A2-A3
Cecilia St B A1
Chamber St F E3
Chancery Lane A E3
Chancery St A D1-E1, E D4-E4, F F2
Chapel Lane E E4-F4
Charlemont Place C C4
Charlemont St C B4
Charles Lane Great B B2
Charles St Great D B2
Charleville Avenue D D2
Chatham St B B3
Chesterfield Av. A A3-B4, F A1-B1
Christ Church Place A D2-E2
Church Av. F C4
Church Road D E3
Church St A C1, E D4, F F1-F2
Church St E. D E3
Church St New F E1
Church St Upper E D4-E3, F F1
City Quay B F1, D C4
Clanbrassil St Lower F F4
Clare Lane B E3
Clare St B E3
Clarence Mangan Road F E4
Clarence Place C E2
Clarendon St B B3
Clareville Grove E D1
Claude Road E E1-F1

Clonliffe Av. D C1-D1
Clonliffe Gardens D C1
Clonliffe Road D B1-C1
Clonmell St C F3
Clyde Road C F4
College Green B B2-C2
College Lane B F2-F3
College St B C1
Constitution Hill E E3
Conyngham Road E A4-B4, F A1
Cook St A C2-D2, F F2
Cope St B B1
Copper Alley A E2, C A1
Cork Hill A F2, C A1
Cork St A A4-B4, F D3-D4
Cornmarket A B2-C2
Cow's Lane A E2
Cowper St E B3
Crane Lane A F2
Crane St F D2
Cranmer Lane C F3
Crawford Av. E F1
Creighton St C E1, D C4
Croker Lane F D2-E2
Cross Kevin St C A2
Crow St B A1-A2
Crown Alley B B1
Cumberland Road C D3
Curry Road F E4
Curved St B A1
Custom House Quay D C4
D'Olier St B C1
Dame Lane A F2, B A2-B2
Dame St A F2, B A2-B2
Daniel St C A3, F F4
Darmouth Road C C4
Davitt Road F A4
Dawson Street B C2-C3, C C1
Dolphin Road F A4-B4
Dolphin's Barn St F C4-D4
Dominick Lane E E3
Dominick St Lower E E3
Donore Av. F D4-E4
Dorset Lane D A2, E F2
Dorset St Lower D A1-A2, E F2
Dorset St Upper E E3-F3
Dowth Av. E C1-C2

LUAS

Liffey. Very comfortable, all double and triple rooms have internet access, tea and coffee facilities. €114–180 (€70 during the week).

The Leeson Inn (C C3)
→ 24 Leeson St Lower
Tel. 662 2002
www.leesoninndowntown.com
Chic, minimalist decor with beautiful touches of gold and silver. Only the noise of traffic – very occasionally – disturbs the quiet of this residential street. Impeccable rooms €119–149 (€ 99 on Sundays).

Temple Bar (B B1)
→ Fleet St. Tel. 677 3333
www.templebarhotel.com
An extremely chic hotel near the artsy cafés of Temple Bar. Air conditioning, beauty salon, refreshments. €120–200.

Albany House (C B3)
→ 84 Harcourt St
Tel. 475 1092
www.dublinhotel

albanyhouse.com
A guesthouse fit for a king. Comfortable rooms with heavy curtains and antique furtniture. Majestic breakfasts of croissants, cheese, cereal and home-baked bread. €160.

LUXURY HOTELS

The Shelbourne (C C2)
→ 27 St Stephen's Green
Tel. 663 4500
www.shelbourne.ie
Tel. 663 4500
www.lemeridien-shelbourne.com
With statues standing at the entrance, the most stunning and beautiful hotel in Dublin has hosted some of Ireland's most significant historical events. Two great bars, a gym and a wonderful 60-ft pool. From €210.

The Gresham (D A3)
→ O'Connell St Upper
Tel. 874 6881

www.gresham-hotels.com
A place of luxury in the midst of the O'Connell St hubbub. Huge reception rooms on the ground floor, with crystal lamps and chandeliers. In the old part of the building, the rooms are like little theaters. Peaceful view over the plane trees. From €350.

The Clarence (A F1)
6-8 Wellington Quay
Tel. 407 0800
www.theclarence.ie
The height of luxury at the heart of the city center, in this hotel belonging to Bono and The Edge of Irish rock group U2. Attractive wood-paneling and some other retro touches avoid the cool elegance of the decor seeming unfriendly in this 'classic-contemporary' setting. The penthouse suite with its own terrace has fantastic views over the city. From €340.

BUS

Principal means of transportation. The bus network is complex and links the whole of the city center and the suburbs. Free maps at the Bus office.

Discounts
For the under 16s, students and families.

Information
→ Dublin Bus Office (**D** A3)
59 Upper O'Connell St
Tel. 873 4222 Mon-Fri 8.30am (9am Fri)–5.30pm; Sat 9.30am–1pm.
www.dublinbus.ie

Timetable
→ Mon-Sat 6am–11.30pm; Sun 9.30am–11.30pm

Nightbuses
→ Thu-Sat midnight–3/4am
Stops at College, D'Olier and Westmoreland streets

Prices
→ Ticket from € 0.95 (available from the bus, but you'll need the exact change ready)
→ One-day ticket €5
→ Three-day ticket €10.50
→ Family one-day ticket €8.50
→ Seven-day pass €20

DART

Dublin Area Rapid Transit. Train serving the suburbs, runs 25 miles along the coast and offers great views. 30 stations, 3 of which are in the center.

Information
→ Tel. 836 6222

Timetable
→ Mon-Sat 6am–midnight; Sun 9am–11.30pm (depart. every 10–15 mins; every 25 mins Sat-Sun)

Ticket price
→ Day ticket €6.80
→ Weekly pass €22.50